STOCK TRADING
MADE SIMPLE

How To Trade on the Stock Market:
The Beginner's Guide

ADE PRESS LTD.
39 Mark Road, Innovation House,
Hemel Hempstead,
HP2 7 DN

Sankar Sharma MSTA, MBA

Learn More About Stock Market Investing And Stock Trading At:

www.RiskRewardReturn.com

For Book Resources go here:

www.riskrewardreturn.com/bookresource

As part of this product you have also received FREE access to the following:

- 'Learn Investing' mini course
- Color charts referenced in 'Stock Trading Made Simple'
- Webinars and Presentations on popular topics of investing and trading

To Gain Access, Simply go to:

www.RiskRewardReturn.com

Wish to progress your learning further?

We have several paid courses available on Investing and Trading.

INVESTING

- Learn At Lunch™ Stock Investing (Beginners)
- 3R Income Accelerator Program (Advanced)

TRADING

- Learn Stock Trading

For All These And Many More Simply Go to:

www.riskrewardreturn.com/learnstockinvesting

www.riskrewardreturn.com/learnstocktrading

Orders: You can also place your order via the email- info@RiskRewardReturn.com

STOCK TRADING MADE SIMPLE - SANKAR SHARMA
How to Trade on the Stock Market: The Beginner's Guide

Publisher: Ade Press Ltd.

Copyright © 2016 by Sankar Sharma

All rights reserved. No part of this book may be reproduced or transmitted in any form or by any means, including electronic, mechanical, photocopying, recording, or by any information storage and retrieval system or otherwise without written permission of the author.

This book may not be lent, resold, hired out or otherwise circulated, disposed of by way of trade in any form of binding or cover other than that in which it is published without the prior consent of the publisher and author.

The right of Sankar Sharma to be identified as the author has been asserted in accordance with the Copyright, Design and Patents Act 1988.

This work is registered with UK Copyright service Registration No: 0284700979

> No responsibility for loss occasioned to any person or corporate body acting or refraining to act as a result of reading material in this book can be accepted by the Publisher or by the Author or by the companies associated with the Author.

STOCK TRADING MADE SIMPLE by SANKAR SHARMA - 1st Edition

ISBN 978-0-9954723-0-3 (Print)

ISBN 978-0-9954723-1-0 (Mobi)

ISBN 979-0-9954723-5-8 (EPUB)

Dedicated to My Beloved Mother.

TABLE OF CONTENTS

Chapter 01: Stock Market Overview ... 9
Chapter 02: Keys to Stock Market Success ... 17
Chapter 03: Strategies ... 15

- Price continuation ... 33
- Assessing the strength of support and resistance lines ... 35
- Four additional ways to identify continuation or reversals of price ... 35
- Trend lines as support and resistance ... 36
  - Strength of the trend ... 38
  - Identifying trend change ... 39
  - Drawing trend lines ... 40
  - Channel Trading ... 40
- Gap as Support and Resistance ... 43
- Fibonacci retracements as Support and Resistance ... 46
- Pivot Point Analysis as Support and Resistance ... 48
- Price Patterns ... 53
- Continuation and Reversal of Price Patterns ... 54
- Major Continuation Patterns ... 55
  - Flags and Pennants ... 55
  - Pennant Example ... 56
  - Triangle Price patterns ... 58
- Wedges ... 65
  - Inverse Head and Shoulders ... 67
- Trading range, congestion or rectangle ... 68
- Single Bottom ... 72
- Double Bottom ... 74
- Triple or Multiple bottom ... 75
  - Single Top ... 76
  - Double Top ... 77

    Triple or Multiple Top 78
    Head and Shoulder Top 79
    Cup and Handle 79
  Volume 80
  Moving averages 81
  Profitable Candlestick Patterns 83

Chapter 04: Shortlisting Stocks **91**

Chapter 05: Pre-Trade Analysis **95**

  PART 1 - Pre-trade Market Analysis Feb 2016 -Checking the Markets and Market SWOT 97

  Market Indices SWOT 98

    Economy Review 104
    Sector Analysis 107
    PART 2 – PRE-TRADE ANALYSIS for Stocks 110
    Trade Validation – Final Checks 110
    Broker Upgrade and Downgrades 110
    Ex-Dividend date 110
    Earnings Announcement 110
    News 111
    Market Open 111
    Volatility 111
    Risk Reward 111
    Annotate the Chart 112
    Confluence 112

  Indicator and Fitness check for the Stock 112

    1. Avoiding chop 112
    2. Buying at a price where sellers are exhausted 112
    3. Volatility indicator Bollinger Bands 114

Chapter 06: Managing Money **117**

Chapter 07: Managing Risk **121**

Chapter 08: Managing the Trade **127**
Chapter 09: Mindset **131**
Chapter 10: Plan, Track and Improve **135**
    Now, let's look at how to create a trading plan. 136
    Trading plan 136
    Annotating Your Journal 139
    Measure to Manage 141
    Post-Trade Analysis 141
Chapter 11: Achieve Stock Market Success **143**
Chapter 12: Afterword **147**
Chapter 13: Bibliography and References **149**
INDEX 150
About the Author 152
Useful Resources @ RiskRewardReturn.com 153

CHAPTER 1

STOCK MARKET OVERVIEW

Why should you invest? An investor goes to the stock market either to grow the money invested, or for income. A company that is publicly held comes to the market to raise money and trades through the exchange or over the counter, to offer equity or share of the company to the investor. When you buy a stock or share, you are actually lending capital to the company to grow its business. You are helping them to expand their products and services, which in turn leads to increased revenue and profit. As an investor, you will own a portion of the company, and hold equity in the company without having to get involved in the day-to-day running of the company. In turn, the company will reward you with a share of its growth, in the form of an increase in the share price or income in the form of dividends (quarterly dividends if you hold American shares).

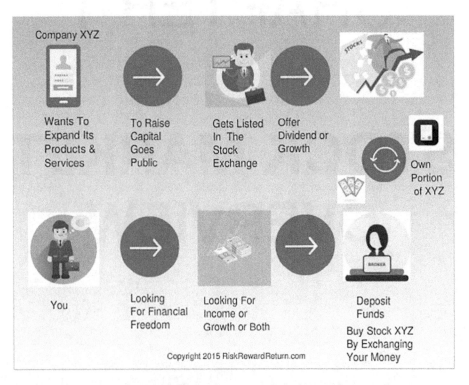

Fig 1.0 Value Exchange between Company and You

It is important to note that it takes companies time to put the borrowed money to work and grow company's research or products or services or exports etc. It takes time for the companies to grow profits. For this reason if you are investor you must exercise patience to see results and growth.

Example is Amazon. Investors in Amazon stock had to wait a good few years and they are now glad they did, as they are sitting on a good increase in profits in their portfolio.

Scope of this book is limited to stocks only. Securities are regulated by FCA (Financial Conduct Authority) in the UK, in America by the SEC (Securities and Exchange Commission) and The Security and Exchange Board of India (SEBI) in India etc.

Markets establish themselves in the form of exchanges. A stock exchange is a place where buyers and sellers of stocks either exchange value or transfer risk. Every buyer needs a seller to sell to and every seller needs a buyer with whom to transfer risk. This is where a broker comes in. Anyone wishing to buy or sell stock needs to find a broker. A broker, dealer or market maker provides transparency and liquidity by finding sellers for buyers, and vice versa. They then trade through the exchange. Examples of exchanges are The New York Stock Exchange (NYSE) in the USA, London Stock Exchange (LSE) in the UK and Bombay Stock Exchange (BSE), NSE the National Stock Exchange in India, Shanghai and Shenzhen Stock exchange in China, Toronto stock exchange in Canada, TSE Tokyo stock exchange in Japan, Deutsche Börse, Hong Kong Stock exchange and Australian Securities exchange to name just a few.

Investors and traders go to the stock market to invest or trade in stocks, bonds, options, exchange traded funds etc. Stocks are often referred to as paper assets. An investor differs from a trader in terms of holding period of a stock. As mentioned before, an investor has a longer term period horizon. Hence, Warren Buffett is often referred to as an investor. On the other hand, a trader takes advantage of short term price movements of the stock to make money. Typically, a swing trader holds their stock for 3 to 7 days, a position trader for a week to a month, and an active investor for months for even years. Some active investors hold their stocks for 1-3 months, from one earnings season to the other. A long term investor holds the stock beyond a year. A day trader holds their position from minutes to hours, and could close their holdings before the end of the day. They often use margin, meaning that they borrow money to trade. Day traders have different capital requirements and rules that they need to adhere to.

If you are beginner in investing, it is strongly advised to stay away from the margin products. Biggest blunder you could make is to go on holiday while you have open margin positions.

As stated earlier, the scope of this book is limited to stocks and does not refer to margin related trading or other asset class trading. The terms investor and trader, investing and trading, invest and trade, stock and share, will be used interchangeably.

Stocks belong to index. When a bunch of stocks are grouped based on Market value or price and the relative value of this group is then measured, it is called an 'index'. The criteria for grouping them is by weighted average capitalization if they are grouped based on Market capitalization. Example for this is S&P 500 which is Market capitalization weighted. In case of Dow Jones 30 index the companies are price weighted. The relative value is called 'points'.

Say you picked and owned a stock in ABC, and by the end of the year you wanted to know if your stock is doing well. Would you agree that you need a benchmark to compare this to? Your index acts as the benchmark. In U.S, S&P 500 is often used as a basis for comparison.

Let's imagine that you purchased an American stock called Walmart (WMT) from the American index. It belongs to the Dow Jones Index. Say after a year you sold it for a 10% gain. During this time, the Dow Index dropped 5%. That means your performance as a stock picker is better than the Dow Jones Index performance. Now imagine that your friend bought an index tracker fund that tracks the Dow Jones Index. He or she could have lost 5% of the investment, and you with your new earned skill have beaten the index tracker fund.

Often, investors use the term market' when they are referring to the major index in their respective country. For example, if an investor in the US says the markets are up today, they mean that the S&P 500 index is up on that day. S&P 500 tracks the collective price movement of the top 500 stocks. The NASDAQ 100 index tracks the top 100 Technology companies in America.

Chapter 1: Stock Market Overview

Fig 1.1 Example of a few major market indices around the world
(This is not an exhaustive list, just to give you a flavor).

UK	US & Canada	EURO	INDIA	CHINA & ASIA
FTSE100	S&P500	Paris CAC40	NIFTY 50	SHANGHAI
FTSE250	DOW 30	Xetra DAX	NIFTY 500	NIKKEI 220
FTSE AIM 100	NASDAQ	MIB30	BSE 100	HANGSENG
FTSE Tec MARK100	RUSSELL2000	SWISS	BSE 500	CSX 300
FTSE Tec MARK100	TSX			ASX 200 (Australia)

Data Courtesy of finviz.com

Index comprises of other things too, including sector and industry groups. In terms of hierarchy, the stock or share is placed into an industry group. An industry group belongs to a sector and the sector belongs to an index. A stock is identified by a ticker symbol. A stock or share is issued by the company. The current price point or value for a stock is called its market value. If you multiply the current price by the number of shares in the market, you will get the market capitalization for that stock.

Fig 1.2 Example of stocks by country, industry group and sector (2016)

Ticker	Company	Sector	Industry	Country	Market Cap	Price	Change
AAPL	Apple Inc.	Consumer Goods	Electronic Equipment	USA	562322.17	101.42	5.32%
ABEV	Ambev S.A.	Consumer Goods	Beverages - Brewers	Brazil	64444.8	4.11	5.93%
AGRO	Adecoagro S.A.	Consumer Goods	Farm Products	Luxembourg	1398.53	11.56	3.96%
BTI	British American Tobacco plc.	Consumer Goods	Cigarettes	United Kingdom	97384.38	103.88	1.75%
CAAS	China Automotive Systems Inc.	Consumer Goods	Auto Parts	China	131.09	4.08	1.75%
COT	Cott Corporation	Consumer Goods	Beverages - Soft Drinks	Canada	1102.38	9.97	1.01%
CPS	Cooper-Standard Holdings Inc.	Consumer Goods	Auto Parts	USA	1206.85	69.24	3.07%
DEO	Diageo plc	Consumer Goods	Beverages - Wineries & Distillers	United Kingdom	67601.9	106.51	2.89%
DLA	Delta Apparel Inc.	Consumer Goods	Textile - Apparel Clothing	USA	101.34	13.11	2.32%
DLPH	Delphi Automotive PLC	Consumer Goods	Auto Parts	United Kingdom	18217.05	65.04	-0.09%

Data Courtesy of finviz.com

You will be buying or selling stocks using online share or stock dealing accounts. At the time of placing a buy or sell order, you will be shown two prices. These are: the ask price (the price at which you can buy the underlying instrument) and the bid price (the price you get when you sell the underlying instrument). The difference between ask price and bid price is called spread.

Entry and exit should be made when the spread is low.

More on buying and selling in the coming chapters. Now continuing on with the index, Dow Jones industrial average (often called DJ30) contains 30 stocks, S&P 500 contains 500 stocks, NASDAQ 100 contains top 100 technology stocks and Russel 3000 contains 3000 small cap American stocks. Most world markets take their cue from US markets. Because of this, if you understand how to invest in American markets, investing in other markets will become fairly easy. In this book, I will be focusing primarily on US markets and other global markets as content warrants.

In regards to US markets, various mutual funds and exchange traded funds (ETFs) track these indices.

An investor can also participate in the ETFs that are linked to sectors, commodities or currencies. In falling markets, some investors use the inverse ETFs to hedge their positions.

For example, inverse ETFs tracking the energy sector will be going up in price, as the sector is falling in price. The reason for bringing up this point is to highlight the fact that an investor can make money in falling markets, and buying an inverse ETF is an easy way to participate and make money in a falling market. Once you understand and master the basics of trading, plenty of opportunities will present themselves for you.

Inverse ETFs are one mode to benefit from, in falling markets.

If you are a beginner and want to get a feel for how short sell (selling first and buying later) works, Inverse ETFs are one way to try it. However; I personally prefer to trade in stocks compared to ETFs. There are lots of other ways to benefit from falling markets, including short selling, usage of options and leveraging instruments; but for the time being these are beyond the scope of this book.

Previously, I mentioned that there are 3000 Russel stocks, 30 Dow stocks, 500 S&P stocks and 100 NASDAQ stocks etc. which are all just in USA. Now, if you add other global indices, the task of finding an opportunity/stock before the next trading day sounds like a gigantic task. How long is it going to take to analyze and find a good stock to invest in? This is where my book will add value.

I have made a sincere attempt to answer 3 key questions in this book.

- How to buy quality stocks
- How to buy low and sell high
- How to control risk in your portfolio and the stock you are buying?

In the next few chapters, I will take you through a step-by-step process on how to master investing and trading. I call this the IVEM process – Identify, Validate, Execute and Measure performance. Once you learn and master this, you will then be equipped to perform LIVE investing or trading with real money.

Actions To Take

1. Find and register with a broker. You need an online 'execution only' broker. Avoid advisory brokers. Preferably a broker who allows you to place stop loss and limit orders.

2. Register with finviz.com to start with as it is free to start with or any other charting software that uses end of day data.
   - Understand the relationship between industry groups, sector and shares.
   - You do not need real-time data for investing, as end of day data will suffice for your investing needs.

3. Go to Yahoo finance or Google finance and explore indices for both local and Global indices.

4. Go to ft.com and read about global economy.

5. Before moving on to the next chapter, take 30 minutes and note down how you would go about picking stocks or how you are currently picking stocks. What is your target, entry and exit criteria? Also, note down any processes that you are currently using.

   For Step 3, 4 and 5, make a one off purchase to get a feel for what is out there, to familiarize and improve your investing vocabulary.

CHAPTER 2

KEYS TO STOCK MARKET SUCCESS

A person who never invested in the stock market often perceives the stock market as a complex, daunting and a gambling kind of place. Because of this perception, they never invest and then get affected by inflation. They don't have their money working for them in the long run. If you are one of them, hopefully; at the end of this book, your perception changes and you start acquiring this new skill of investing in the stock market. The subject will no longer be daunting once you familiarize yourself with the terminology, methods and spend time acquiring the knowledge required to be self-sufficient and dedicate adequate practice time for investing in the stock market.

It might feel like it is a gigantic mountain to climb. It can be overwhelming at times! However, if you have a step-by-step process and a detailed road map for mastering trading and investment, you too can achieve success given time.

The step-by-step process includes: Step 1 – Identification, Step 2 – Validation, Step 3 – Execution and Step 4 – Measure Performance. This is shown in Fig.2.1, titled 'Steps to achieving stock market success.'

To be able to successfully implement this process, you need to acquire some new skills. These include:

- Shortlisting stocks – filtering trades based on a criteria.
- Pre-trade analysis – to identify possible opportunities, headwinds that could cause stress and turbulence, ways to validate the opportunities identified using strategies, filtering your choices for quality, high probability stocks to invest in.
- Strategies – to help in finding possible price points for entry and exit with an intent to buy low and sell high.
- Trading plan – learning the art of preparing a trade plan that could guide in times of panic or emotion. A trade plan is like a business plan. Trading is your business.
- Managing money – capital management.
- Managing risk – assessing, controlling risk and rewards.
- Managing trade – to maximize profits and minimize loss.

Chapter 2: Keys to Stock Market Success

- Mindset – learning discipline and having the ability to control emotions like fear and greed. Often referred to as 'Trading Psychology'
- Post-trade analysis – to assess what you could have done, should have done, lessons learnt, what you could start doing and what you could stop doing etc.
- Measure to manage – learn to measure and manage so that you can minimize the deviation between what was planned and what was achieved.
- Maintain a journal – learning organisation principles such as maintaining a journal to identify what worked and what did not, reasons for entering or exiting a trade, and time horizons.

Once you specialize and master the above skills, then you can start implementing them in the four step process of Identification, Validation, Execution and Measure Performance.

Step 1 – Identification

You can use shortlisting stocks and pre-trade analysis to spot opportunities and threats in the domestic and global market places. These can be short, medium or long term opportunities. At this stage you will not know whether it is time to get involved in an opportunity, or react to the threats. You need to validate them to see if they are viable, assess risk and return, and find out when exactly to invest. This is step 2.

Step 2 – Validation

You need to learn to validate the opportunities that you have spotted in Step 1. For validation, you will incorporate strategies (by using technical analysis, one of the effective ways to analyze markets or stock) that will help you with high probability entries and exits, levels to exit on profit (targets) and levels to exit when wrong (stop loss).

Technical analysis is a method that is simple, effective, easy to learn and adopt, compared to other methods like Fundamental analysis or Value analysis techniques. By making use of various techniques that will be discussed in the chapter on strategies, you can validate each of your stock selection. You can then filter and focus on a handful of quality stocks to trade, in line with your investing timeframe. Remember that trading is an emotional transaction, and emotions like fear and greed could lead you to make mistakes. This is where Step 3 comes in.

Step 3 – Execution

As soon as you purchase a stock a few things happen. 1) The stock price may jump higher and you are in profit. 2) Price may go down that means you are now taking risk. 3) Price goes nowhere. Now it prompts you to make a decision whether to sell or wait for more increase in price or buy more of the same stock. Psychologically this triggers two emotions Fear of losing your investment, Greed.

This is where learning, How to manage risk, manage money, and manage trade could help. Risk Management is to deal with 'Losses', Money Management is to 'Protect Capital' and Trade Management is to do with 'Order Placing' .These topics are covered in greater detail in the coming chapters.

Step 4 – Measure Performance

Once you have exited the trade by selling your shares purchased, you have either profit, loss or break even. If you wish to improve your outcome, then you need to measure your validation and execution process using post-trade analysis. If you have any findings, then record them as feedback. This will allow you to improve your validation and execution skills. Repeated mistakes will go back into the trading plan as rules to prevent reoccurrence. Maintaining a journal to record all of your trading activity is one of the key components of the 'measure performance' process. Any findings that come out of the 'measure performance' will now become new rules or amendments to existing rules in your trading plan (What goes in a good Trading plan is discussed in detail in the coming chapters). You need to take steps to improve on the process of validation and execution in your next trade. Continue the process of step 1 to 4 with feedback and improvements, until you have mastered the execution process.

Chapter 2: Keys to Stock Market Success

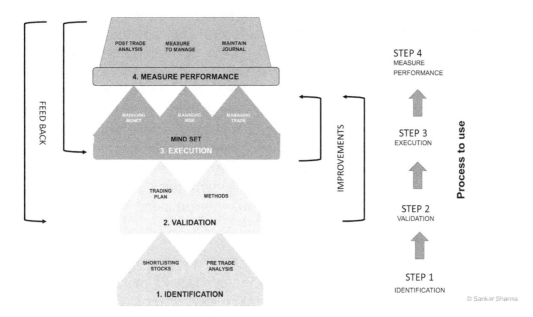

Fig 2.1 Step-by-Step process for a Beginner Investor

Once you become accustomed to the step-by-step process, you will then learn to spot any opportunities and threats. Once you have identified these, don't immediately jump to act. You need a time trigger to buy or sell. This is where learning and mastering Technical analysis will be an effective and powerful tool for a beginner investor. It will allow you to be on the correct side of the markets. It is not mandatory for you to precisely predict the turning points. Staying on the correct side of the market using what you learn in Technical analysis, using risk control techniques, working out targets (before even entering the trade) based on price patterns, applying a profit maximization strategy and picking stocks that give twice the rewards for the amount at risk is more than adequate for a beginner to be making returns in the stock market.

Many investors and traders keep searching for a holy grail or the next best automated system or perfect system. There isn't one. Don't waste your time looking for it. No method or trading system is perfect and losses or drawdowns are inevitable. Losses are part of the investing business. That is why learning how to manage Risk Management will help you to control your losses.

As mentioned before, in order to excel and be consistent in your returns, you must learn discipline, manage or control risk not only in individual position you hold but also control risk in the portfolio (collection of your investments), manage money and manage trade. Be disciplined enough to stick to the rules of the method. You must not intervene with the trade execution process by moving the stops or exiting too soon. Psychology plays an important role, since trading or investing is an emotional activity. The more you learn about yourself and your reaction and relationship to money, the more successful you will become in managing your trade, in order to achieve consistent returns. You will learn quickly that if you develop tenacity when market goes against you, then sticking to the rules and process, will reward you handsomely.

If you are not achieving consistent returns with your investments or trading, then it is very likely that you are still in the process of mastering the areas mentioned above. You may not have taken one or more of the following, i.e. risk management, money management, trade management, profit maximization techniques or mindset into consideration. I am deliberately repeating these because they are very important and you must pay attention to them.

Professional investors excel in paying particular attention to their mindset, managing risk and managing trade and strategies. Additionally, they cultivate the habit of recording their trades, reasons for buying and selling; and their wins and losses. They study these results and take corrective steps to improve. A great way to improve and accelerate your learning is to have mentors who will help you accelerate your learning and cross the hurdles you face along the way. Also, trading alongside a buddy or in a group helps both sides.

Chapter 2: Keys to Stock Market Success

Actions To Take

1. In the last chapter, you did a 30 minute exercise on how to go about your stock picking process. So, after reading this chapter, if you noticed items that were not in your list, include them and highlight them as important.

2. If you have had investments in the past, you could check them against the steps mentioned here and see if any of these steps could have helped you to avoid or minimize loss, or make more profit.

3. Using the financial press or media, note 3 stocks that went up in price and another 3 that went down. Make note of the stock names and use this in your charting software. Write five reasons why you think, the price has gone up or down. Once you complete the book revisit and see how the lessons from the coming chapters make a difference. It is a good way to measure your progress, before and after.

CHAPTER 3

STRATEGIES

Deciding precisely, when to enter and when to exit the stock market is extremely hard. Technical analysis is an effective way to analyze the markets or stocks. It will provide you with a road map, which can be used to chalk out future price trends or movements. Prices are represented in the form of charts. Like airfares going up when the demand is high, the price of a stock moves up when the demand is high. This is represented by an increase in buying volume. Now, let me put this in the investing context. The movement of price is called price action. The point where demand starts to increase, and price stops falling and starts to rise, is called 'support' or 'floor' (Fig 3.1 Resistance or Support). At the point where the price is too high, the demand starts to dry out. The price stops going up, and starts to stall and fall. This is called 'resistance' or 'ceiling'. When you plot price as a dot, and volume as a bar for each day on the y-axis against time (date) on the x-axis, you will get a price chart. When you start connecting these price points, you will get a line chart. Histograms below the price are volume histograms. If sellers are dominant then volume of sellers is shown in darker shade.

Now, if you replace price dots with a vertical line, the top end of the line represents the highest price that it reached that day (price high) and the bottom end represents the lowest it recorded that day (price low). You now have a high-low price bar.

If you take each day's vertical line and try to add in a bit more detail, by means of adding a horizontal tip to the vertical line to signify the price at which the day started - open price and a right horizontal tip to show the price at which the day ended. You now have 4 price points on each of the lines. Each line represents the open price, close price, high price and low price. Now this is a bar chart. Fig 3.2.a

Chapter 3: Strategies

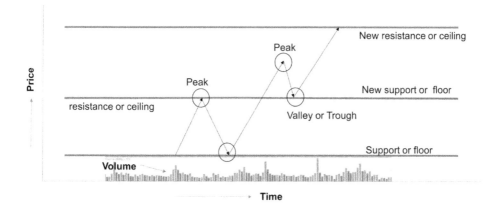

Fig 3.1 Resistance or Support

If you connect the open and close prices with a rectangle and leave the rest of the line on either side, you have a candle. The rectangle connecting open and close is called the body, and the extensions either side that represent high and low are called the wick. If you draw the up price candles as empty candles, and down candles filled, you now have a candlestick chart.

Fig 3.2.a gives a clear visual representation of two chart types - Bar Chart and candlestick chart. Charts used in this book are either bar chart or candlestick chart. Candles with a white body or hallow going up like balloons represent raising price, and are often referred to as bullish candles. Candles shown in the figure below filled are like iron rods falling and are often referred to as bearish candles.

Fig 3.2.a. Bar Chart and Candlestick Chart

Imagine that a day's price movement was plotted both as a bar as well as a candle and Close price is above the Open, then we say the price for the Day is 'Up' (Refer to Fig. 3.2.b that shows how a raising price represented as a bar and the same represented in a candlestick format)

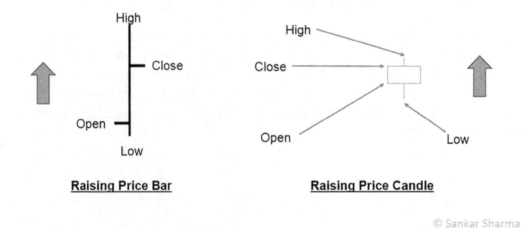

Fig 3.2.b. Raising Price Bar vs Raising Price Candle

Chapter 3: Strategies

Again imagine that one single day's price movement is plotted both as a bar and as a candle. If Close price for the day is less than the Open price for the day we say we had a 'Down' Day (Refer to Fig. 3.2.c that shows how a falling price represented as a bar and the same represented in a candlestick format)

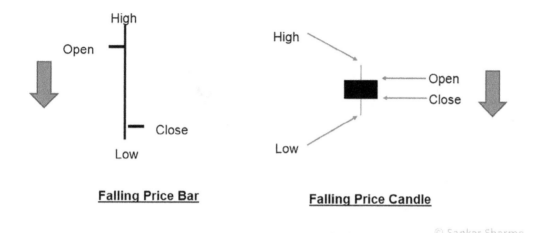

Falling Price Bar   Falling Price Candle

© Sankar Sharma

Fig 3.2.c. Falling Price Bar vs Falling Price Candle

Where is support and where is resistance? How do you identify them so that you can buy at the lowest price where price stops falling and starts to raise? How do you identify the point to sell where price is perceived high? To identify this support area or support zone, and resistance area or resistance zone, you need to identify peaks and troughs.

Peak and troughs are often referred to as reaction high or reaction low respectively. The peaks that create major swings are called swing highs and the same applies to swing lows.

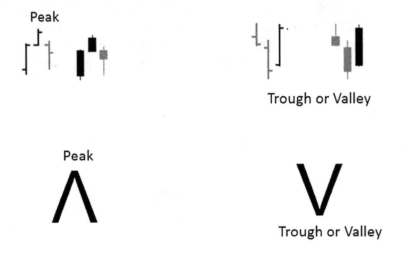

Fig 3.3.a. Peak and Trough

A peak is a bar or candle that has a higher high than the bar before it and the bar after it. A trough has a lower low compared to the bar that preceded it and the bar that succeeds it.

When you connect at least two troughs or one peak and one trough using a horizontal line, you get the support zone.

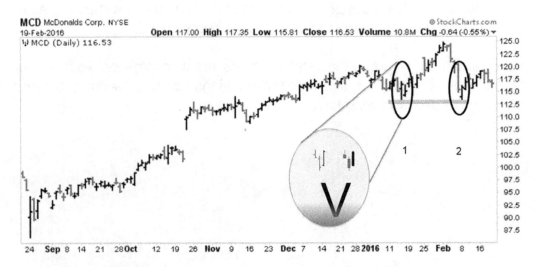

Fig 3.3.b. Support Zone – Joining Two Troughs

You can mark the support zone with a green line (Refer Fig 3.3.b for Support Zone).

Joining at least two peaks via a horizontal line will give a resistance line, and you can color this red for easy identification. (Refer Fig 3.3.c for Resistance Zone)

Fig 3.3.c. Resistance Zone – Join Two Peaks

The distance that price travels from trough to peak is called 'Up swing', and from peak to trough, is called 'Down Swing'. (Refer Fig. 3.3.d Kellogg's price char). This is because price swings from trough to peak and vice versa. In order to draw support and resistance lines, you need to focus on the peak or trough that had maximum swing lengths. In other words, you need to look for swing pivots that are generating maximum reaction.

Fig 3.3.d Up Swing and Down Swing

If you refer to the Amazon chart in Fig 3.3.e, you will notice the peak and the trough (valley) circled. Note the volume, the buying volume is right below the arrow that says conservative entry. When price breaks the resistance line at $580, the resistance (identified by red line) becomes support (line color changed to Green to indicate it has now become support). The same support again becomes resistance as the price goes down, at the price point $580 on the extreme right of the chart.

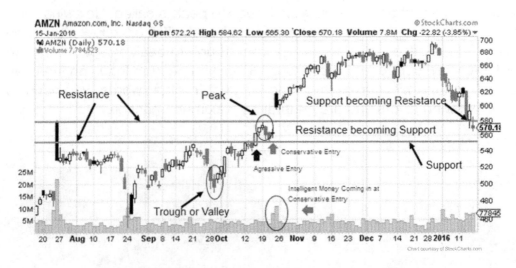

Fig 3.3.e. Peak and Trough, Resistance and Support

Chapter 3: Strategies

When the price breaks through its nearest resistance zone, it comes back to create a trough in the same zone, before stopping and continuing its original course. The resistance zone then becomes its new support zone and vice versa. You need to remember to change the color on your chart to capture this. Support Zones are drawn in Green color and Resistance in red. When Support becomes resistance then change the color from green to red and vice versa.

Even though you draw support and resistance by joining two points, they are actually zones, so do not restrict yourself to the line you need to treat it as a zone. When price is starting to approach the resistance zone or support zone, two things can happen. Either the price will continue its trend, or it will stop and reverse. This is represented in Fig 3.4.

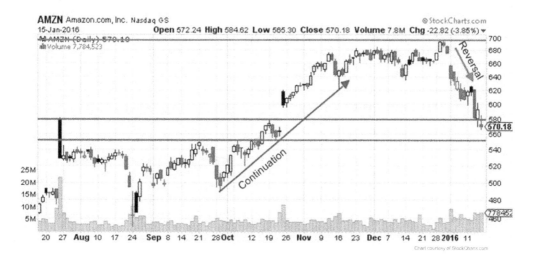

Fig 3.4 Price Continuation and Price Reversal

Price continuation

Consider the case of a Resistance zone, price sometimes pierces through the resistance and continues its trend upwards (Fig 3.4). If this happens, you have what is called a 'break out'. You then have two places to enter the trade (or buy the stock). One comes immediately as soon as the price pierces the resistance zone. This will be an aggressive entry point (aggressive entry because it has higher profit potential but also it is high risk because this could be a false breakout meaning it could reverse and make loss). The second is when the price pierces through the resistance zone, and then comes back to test it. This time the zone becomes a support zone, and the price starts to react and continue its journey upwards. This point will be a conservative entry (Ref Fig 3.3.e for Aggressive and conservative entry points), and you will be entering on the bounce. This point risk is low because you can place your stop below the point where it bounced recently. There is also a third entry possible; this happens when the price breaks the nearest peak or swings high.

Price reversal

Price gets rejected at the resistance zone and bounces in the opposite direction to its original course, like a tennis ball returning from the ceiling when thrown upwards (Fig 3.4). In this case, you should wait for the peak confirmation i.e. swing high, before the price starts to break the low price of the trough. Aggressive entry is right at the resistance point. As an investor, if you bought the stock and your account type doesn't permit short selling, then these reversal points will be nothing but points where you will sell and exit the trade or trim your holdings.

Assessing the strength of support and resistance lines

When price comes to either support or resistance, there is always a doubt whether it is going to hold and go in the direction that you expect it to. In the absence of any other techniques, to get confirmation and assurance, you need to look for confluence. In this case, you could use candlestick patterns and volume in order to do this. Later chapters will give you more ways to confirm and validate entry and exit points.

For a resistance to hold, you should expect a bearish candlestick pattern and price falling with increased selling volume. Most charting software will have the buying volume, selling volume or dollar volume shown below the price, to indicate if it is buying volume or selling volume. Usually, selling volume is marked in red color or dark shade. If the price is coming up to the resistance, you can expect the buying volume to slow down and the selling volume to pick up. Exit the buy position only after you have a confirmed peak.

Similarly, if price is coming down to the support line, you need a confirmed trough or bottom, a price pattern like double bottom that looks like a 'W', a bullish candlestick pattern (like a hammer or a bullish engulfing candle etc.), and an increase in buying volume. More on the price patterns and candlestick patterns in the coming chapters.

In summary, here are the steps for drawing support and resistance zones. The same rules will be applied in drawing trend lines. Trend lines are inclined support and resistance lines.

STEP 1: From the current price point, look to the left of the chart and mark at least two troughs to draw the support line/zone (if you can't see the second point, try to zoom out of the chart so that you can see more price action on the chart).

STEP 2: From the current price point, look left of the chart and mark at least two peaks or tops to draw the resistance line/zone (if you can't see the second point, try to zoom out of the chart).

Remember to pick the peaks or troughs that had a maximum swing.

STEP 3: If you have more than two touches, make the line thicker to indicate that it is a strong support/resistance zone.

STEP 4: Take note of the price at the support zone as a potential buy point, and the nearest resistance zone as your possible first target.

STEP 5: Mark volume and candlestick patterns.

STEP 6: Now repeat the exercise three more times.

Four additional ways to identify continuation or reversals of price

You noted in the last section that support and resistance zones help to identify price reaction zones, where price could either continue or reverse. There are 5 other techniques you can use to identify support and resistance, just by using price. These are:

- Trend lines.
- Gap.
- Fibonacci.
- Pivot Point Analysis.
- Price Patterns.

Actions To Take

1. Using the financial press or media, note three stocks that went up in price and another three that went down. Make note of the stock name and with the help of your charting software, start drawing support and resistance lines. Examine how the price reacts at these zones.
2. Create a portfolio list (most websites allow you to create and track portfolios) for support and resistance, and monitor these over the next three months.
3. Repeat this exercise until you reach the next section.

Trend lines as support and resistance

Trend lines are drawn exactly the same way, with the same rules that you have used to draw support and resistance lines, except that trend lines are inclined. You now have a good idea of a peak or the top as some call it, and you know how to identify the trough, valley or bottom. Now you need to understand what a trend is, and how to identify if the stock is in an uptrend or downtrend.

If the stock price starts to make higher peaks and higher troughs, or higher tops and higher bottoms, then the stock is in an uptrend. In other words, if the current price peak is higher than the previous peak, and the price keeps making higher highs and higher lows, the stock is considered to be in an uptrend. (Ref. Fig 3.5.Identification of trend).

Chapter 3: Strategies

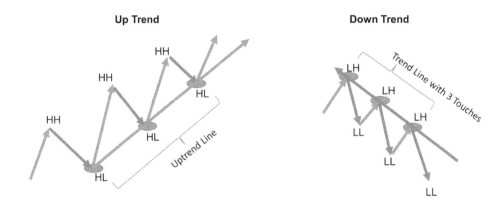

Fig 3.5 Identification of a Trend

If the price starts making lower peaks and lower troughs, in other words, lower highs and lower lows, then the price is trending down or the stock is in a downtrend.

To declare that a stock is beginning its uptrend, the price of the stock must make at least one higher high and one higher low. For the downtrend, the price must make at least one lower high and one lower low.

It is important to note that when a stock is strongly trending up, the primary trend is up (Ref. Fig 3.6. Primary and Secondary Trend). When the price returns towards the trend line from its recent high, you have a secondary trend in the opposite direction, and a pull back to the trend line before it breaks the trend line, or resumes the trend in the direction of the primary uptrend. This is also the case in a downtrend.

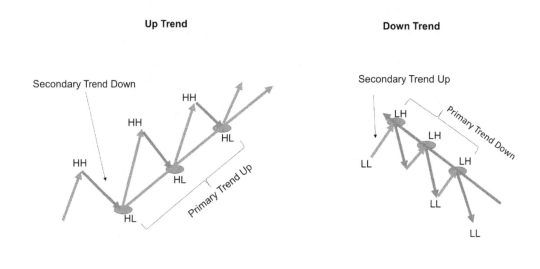

Fig 3.6 Primary and Secondary Trend

Strength of the trend

The stronger the ascent of the trend line, the stronger the trend is.

Imagine that the stock started its trend at an ascent of 30 degrees to the support line, as shown in (Ref. Fig 3.7 Strength of the trend). Now, if the price trend gets stronger, you might find a newer trend that is steeper than the original trend.

As the trend line becomes steeper, it also becomes less sustainable.

It is worth mentioning that if one of the peaks you used for drawing the trend line coincides with the peak of the resistance zone or line, this price point is considered as a higher probability resistance point, and you must highlight or make note of it in your analysis. Similarly, if the trough you used for the trend line support coincides with a support zone, then this price becomes a high probable support Point and also a point of confluence.

AEP Industries chart (Ref. Fig. 3.7), shows how the original trend changed to a steeper uptrend around October 2015. From raising the angle of trend, you can conclude that the trend is getting steeper. The steeper the angle of the trend, the less stable the trend will be.

Fig 3.7 Strength of the Trend

Identifying trend change

Imagine a stock in an uptrend. In this case, imagine the price fails to make a new peak or new higher high. Instead, the price makes a first new lower high. Now, it is time to consider tightening the stop or exiting the position. As soon as the price makes its first new lower low, you can confirm that the uptrend is no longer in force.

Similarly, if the price is in a downtrend, and then makes its first higher high and higher low, you can confirm the end of downtrend. This does not constitute an immediate change to the opposite trend. It's quite possible that the price may be resting here, going sideways. If you are unable to spot the peaks and troughs then you may want to temporarily switch your candlestick chart to a line chart, and mark higher high as HH and Lower high as LH, lower low as LL and Higher Low as HL, before reverting back to candlestick or bar chart, and aligning the line.

Fig 3.8 Identifying Trend Change

In the Apple (AAPL) Stock (Fig. 3.8 Identifying trend change), you can see how the uptrend is highlighted, making new higher highs and higher lows. The stock then breaks the trend line in mid-November and makes a lower low, followed by a lower high in early December, confirming that the uptrend is no longer active. In the 3rd week of December 2015, you can see lower high and lower lows, confirming the downtrend.

Drawing trend lines

To draw a trend line you need at least two touches. These are either the peaks, or lower highs that you join for a downtrend line. To draw an uptrend line you need three troughs or three higher lows. More touches means more strength in the trend. Recent touches should be given utmost importance, and if a trend line is extending for a longer period, it will be considered a stronger trend line. Most beginners try to connect it to the current price. Avoid making this mistake. A trend line is drawn connecting peaks or troughs and not to the recent price you see on the price chart. A trend line drawn horizontally is nothing but a support and resistance line.

Channel Trading

Whenever there is an uptrend line or down trend line, it is always a good idea to draw a parallel trend line to the original drawn. This will show you whether there are any channel trading possibilities available for the stock. If

Chapter 3: Strategies 41

you carefully notice the Boeing (BA) price chart (Fig. 3.9 Price Channel – Up Side), you could see the Buy points where the stock could be purchased with low risk. Reward is the upper trend line (acting as resistance). You could also see the couple of Sell points marked as the price touched the Upper trend line resistance. Also, notice how buyer volume started to support these low risk buy points. This indicates a good set of confluences.

Fig 3.9 Price Channel- Up Channel

If you notice in the Apple (AAPL) chart (Fig 3.10 price channel), there is a nice downward channel. The top and bottom of the channel become resistance and support respectively for the stock. If the channel is uptrending in the direction of the trend, buy at the support and sell at the top channel line. In a downtrend, every time price reaches the top channel sell, buy it back at the bottom. In case of Apple (AAPL), every time the price reached Lower High (LH), advanced traders would sell short and buy it back when price makes Lower Low (LL) to make a lot of money, in a short period of time. Even though it is too advanced for a beginner at this stage, I just want you to be aware of the possibilities that exist beyond buying and selling a share. In summary it is possible to make money when price starts to fall in a stock.

Fig 3.10 Price Channel – Down Channel

How long can trends last? Well, this largely depends on the strength of the trend and how good your research and analysis is in spotting one. Here is an example: look at the Chart of O'Relly Automotive, Inc. in Fig 3.11. The stock went from $4.12 in the year 2000, to $277 in November 2015. It went from approximately $25 in 2009 to $277 in 2015.

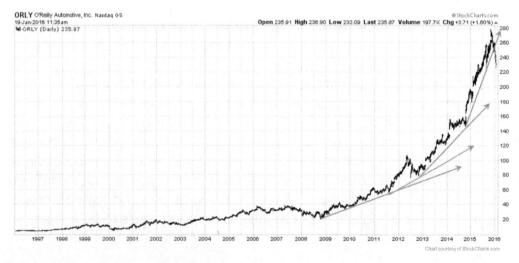

Fig 3.11 Trend Duration

Chapter 3: Strategies

> **Actions To Take**
>
> 1. From the financial press or media, pick five new stocks that went up in price and another five that went down. Make note of the stock and with the help of your charting software, start drawing trend lines and channels in addition to marking support and resistance zones. As the price approaches the support and resistance zones, observe how the price reacts at these zones.
> 2. Identify buy and sell points, identify confluence points, strength of trend, and trend direction change.
> 3. Create a portfolio list for trending stocks. Monitor them over the next three months.
> 4. Repeat this exercise until you reach the next section.

Gap as Support and Resistance

A gap is created when the stock price jumps and opens at a higher or lower price point than expected. A gap opening could act as support or resistance as long as the gap is not filled.

If a stock gaps up, the gap opening may act as support. If price ever comes back to that level, the probability of the support holding is very high on the first attempt. In the case of Mattel (MAT) Stock (Ref. Fig. 3.12a Gap up opening acting as a Support Zone), the gap opening acts as a support zone.

Fig 3.12.a Gap up opening acting as a Support Zone

If the price gaps down, the gap opening will act as resistance. If the price tries to come back to that level, the probability of the support holding is very high on the first attempt. In the case of Apple (AAPL) stock (Refer to figure 3.12b Gap down opening acting as a Resistance Zone), the gap down opening acts as a resistance zone.

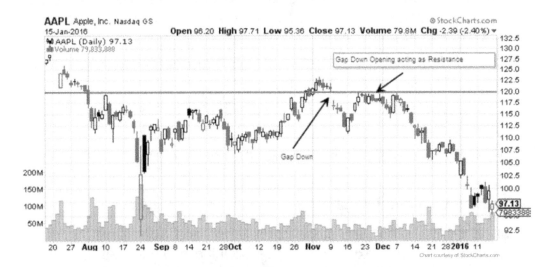

Fig 3.12.b Gap down opening acting as a Resistance Zone

During recent years, an interesting second pattern has emerged around the gaps, (Ref. Fig 3.13 Previous Support acting as a stronger Resistance) where sometimes the price struggles to go past the previous support line. This is true especially when the support happens to be in the gap. This is evident in the Barracuda networks (CUDA) price chart. Instead of the gap down opening acting as resistance, the previous support acts as stronger resistance.

Chapter 3: Strategies

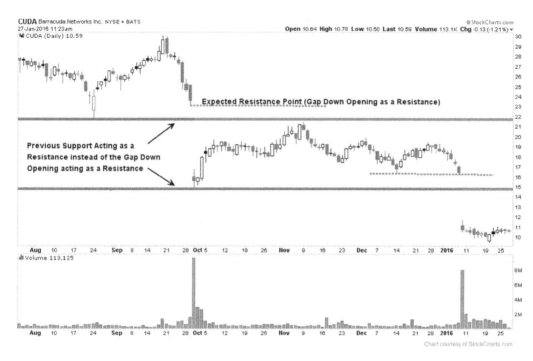

Fig 3.13 Previous Support acting as a stronger Resistance

It is also worth noting that a stock that had a gap in price for the first time, could gap two more times. There is no guarantee of anything in the markets, but there is a high probability. The first time that a stock gaps is known as the 'break out gap'. The second time it gaps is known as the 'continuation gap'; this often happens in the direction of the first gap. This is followed by the last gap, called an 'exhaustion gap'.

Actions To Take

1. From the financial press or media, note three stocks that gapped up in price and another three that gapped down. Draw gap up open support and gap down open resistance points, along with normal support and resistance zones.

2. Create a portfolio list for gap stocks. Monitor them over the next three months.

3. Repeat this exercise until you reach the next section.

Fibonacci retracements as Support and Resistance

Fibonacci was the nickname of the 12th Century Italian Mathematician, Leonardo Pisano. He introduced 'The Fibonacci sequence', 1, 1, 2, 3, 5, 8, 13, 21, 34, 55, 89…etc. As per the sequence, you add the 1st and 2nd numbers to get the third number, and the 3rd and 4th to get the fifth, and so on. Similarly if you divide 89 by 55, 55 by 34, 34 by 21, 21 by 13 etc. you get 1.618033, which is often called the 'Golden Ratio'. The number of petals on a flower, the number of spirals in a pineapple, and many others, all represent the Fibonacci sequence. It is the golden ratio and Fibonacci sequence that inspired mathematicians to apply these concepts to the financial markets. You will be wise to use Fibonacci as a confluence study when used along with others. Do not solely depend on it. Fibonacci works well with volume profile than on its own.

Drawing Fibonacci retracements will help you to spot potential turning points in a stock. As a rule of thumb for an up trending stock, you should draw from the most recent lowest low on the chart, to the most recent highest high on the chart. This will allow you to see where the secondary trend is going to stop, and where the price could bounce back. Remember you are interested in the first touch of these levels only, and you want to see a pivot form before entering the trade, along with other confluences like buying volume on the stock. You are looking at buy volume increase, because the stock comes down to the Fibonacci levels from its uptrend. The most widely followed levels are 38%, 50% and 62% retracements.

In markets like oil, some traders use variations of these levels. However, these are quite advanced, and beyond the scope of this book. You should use Fibonacci with confluence, and not on its own. For stocks in uptrend, pick the recent highest high and pick the lowest low for the time period (say 6 month chart showing daily price action). Start drawing from the low point to the high. Most software follows this method. For a down trending stock, the drawing method is the exact opposite to that of up trending stock.

Chapter 3: Strategies 47

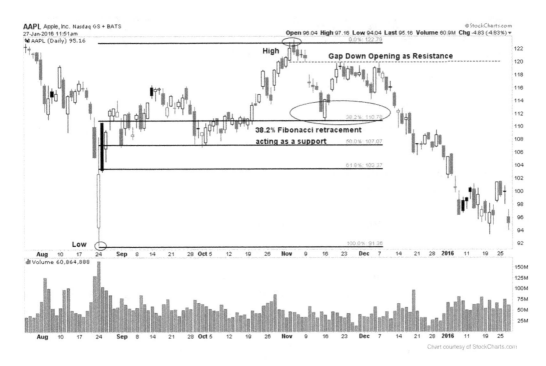

Fig 3.14 Using Fibonacci as support

If you notice in the Apple (AAPL) chart (Fig 3.14 using Fibonacci as support), Fibonacci lines were drawn after the price gapped down. It is important to know where the price is going to find support and reverse. To draw the Fibonacci lines, the nearest highest high price of 122.98 and the lowest low available in recent times (which is at 92.21) was chosen. That gave 3 possible reversal points. $110.78 at 38.2%, $107.07 at 50% and $103.37 at 61.8% level. Look at the first touch reversal, which actually took place with a nice trough or pivot at the price level of 110.78. Now, you already knew beforehand that there is a gap resistance sitting at approximately $120 level. Knowing this, you could have bought this share at $110.78 with a stop of $109 (if it went below 110.78 you know that 38.2% level did not hold and the stock is heading for may be 50% level) and a target of $120. This represents a very good risk to reward trade. Now you can see how it is all starting to come together.

> **Actions To Take**
> 1. Select any three stocks and start drawing Fibonacci zones.
> 2. Identify 38.2%, 50% and 61.8% zones, mark them on the chart and save the chart.
> 3. Watch over a 3 month period to see how various stocks react to these levels.
> 4. Repeat this exercise until you reach the next section.

Pivot Point Analysis as Support and Resistance

Pivot point analysis is a time tested strategy for identifying possible targets and entries. Many uninformed investors fail to take advantage of this. If you haven't been using pivot levels or have not heard of this before, then it is high time you add it to your strategies. This will work on any stock with high liquidity or volume. Pivot point levels help you to quickly identify potential support and resistance zones. (Ref. Fig. 3.15.c Chipotle Pivot Levels – 29-Jan-2016)

Always try using pivot levels on the current time frame you are analyzing and a time frame above it. Examine and see whether price reacts better to the current time frame pivot levels or one level higher time frame pivot levels. In other words, if you are using a daily price chart for analysis, try using weekly pivot levels on the daily chart and see how price reacts at these levels. For some stocks, the weekly levels may work better on daily time frame. Validate this by checking if it worked before. If it did then you are good to use weekly pivots for this stock on daily time frame.

The idea is to look for confluence, in order to increase the probability in your favor. (More factors lining up increasing probability.)

Prices react at pivot levels. When you plot the pivot points, you get 5 lines on the chart. These are the pivot line or level denoted as (P), Resistance 1 line or level (R1), Resistance 2 line (R2), Support line 1 (S1) and Support line 2 (S2). You can also have Resistance 3 (R3) and Support 3 (S3). It is not uncommon for traders to use mid-levels between P and R1, R1 and R2 etc. as additional levels.

Several variations of pivot point calculations are available. Some include open price, and some exclude open price. However, the most commonly used formula is referred to in Figure 3.15.a. The only difference is that on gap day/week, you should change your calculation for the pivot line (P). So, the pivot line in this case is

Pivot line = (previous day's high (H), low (L), close (C) and the gap day open price)/4.

The same rule applies to all of the timescales, including the higher time frame relative to the current. You will be amazed when you see it in action. Any method, study or indicator you add; always validate it by checking to see if it worked in the past, for that stock.

Level	Calculation when there is No Gap in Price
H=High, L=Low, C=Close	
P (Pivot Line)	=(H+L+C)/3
R1 (Resistance 1)	=P+H-L
R2 (Resistance 2)	=2XP-L
R3 (Resistance 3)	=H+2X(P-L)
S1 (Support 1)	=(PX2)-H
S2 (Support 2)	=P-H+L
S3 (Support 3)	=L-2X(H-P)

Fig 3.15.a. Pivot point calculation

Again in the case of Chipotle (CMG) stock, current pivot lines are shown as P, R1, R2, S1 and S2 plotted on the daily time frame. Look to the left of the chart (Fig 3.15.b Chipotle Pivot Levels 15-Jan-2016) and see if the previous pivot levels worked. If they did, there is a good probability that the new levels will work. In the case of Chipotle (CMG), you can see that the levels worked in the past. This fact was highlighted in the chart by the arrows. Now, it is important to remember that pivot lines, P, S1, S2, R1, and R2 etc. act like magnets. You can see that this is happening with Chipotle. Unfortunately, there is no holy grail and no single method or indicator that works 100%. Hence the reason for looking at confluence i.e. stacking probabilities in your favor.

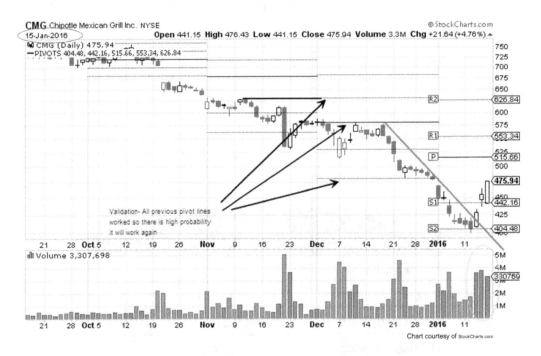

Fig 3.15.b. Chipotle Pivot Levels 15-Jan-2016

In the Chipotle (CMG) case, it broke the trend line and the volume was excellent. It is also worth noting that on the daily chart (Fig 3.15.b), the current price is at 475.94 and the nearest resistance is at $480, the previous pivot line. The pivot line at $480 was a previous support. As the price broke below it, the price point $480 has now become a new resistance (Fig 3.15.c Chipotle Pivot Levels – 29-Jan-2016). It will remain so until it is broken to the upside.

So, how can I show you how a trade works? How do I demonstrate this in the absence of a live interaction? The idea is to build confidence in what you are learning. For this, I have included snap shots of Chipotle stocks between 15 Jan 2016 (Fig 3.15 b) and Jan 29th (Fig 3.15c). (Snapshot representing two different points of time). You can see how these levels worked well. Incidentally the $480 level also happens to be a gap down

Chapter 3: Strategies

opening resistance, another confluence point. (Confluence of various studies indicates or supports the buy or sell decision).

Any instruments, shares or asset classes or indices or assets discussed in this book are for educational purposes only and must not be treated as investment advice.

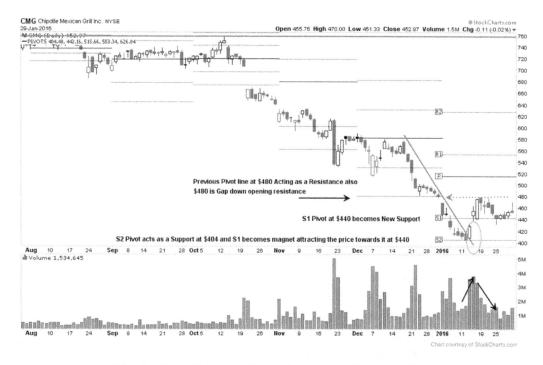

Fig 3.15.c. Chipotle Pivot Levels – 29-Jan-2016

Before moving on to the next method, let's check if all of the strategies that I have discussed so far are working. Here is another case study to build your confidence in the strategies. No indicators are used, so they are all purely based on price. The plan is to use price, volume, support and resistance, trend lines, (gaps if they exist) and pivot lines. The idea is to look for a place of confluence, high probability entry and high probability exit. By stacking probabilities (confluence), you want to buy a stock at low price and sell high with higher probability of success.

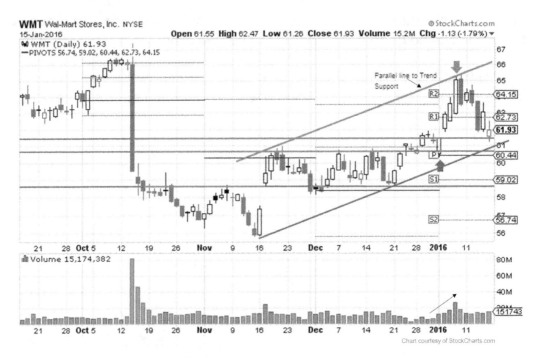

Fig 3.16.a Case Study - Walmart

If you examine the price chart for Walmart (WMT) in Fig 3.16.a, you will notice the channel lines (Two parallel tend lines). When price touches the bottom of the channel and bounces back upwards you have support troughs. Now when you add pivots and look for points of confluence, high probable entry points, you notice a good entry point at 60.44 price (where the up arrow is placed). It is the entry. The price pierced through the near resistance, and came back to test the support, with the buying volume increasing at the same time coinciding with the Pivot at 60.44 (marked as P). This implies we have multiple confirmations and a high probable entry at 60.44. Now you need to look for a place to exit or take some portion of your profit and capital off. Daily Pivot level Resistance R1 and Resistance R2 will give two such price points where you would like to move your stop to. You also know that price is likely to reverse at the upper channel line and you could exit portion of your holdings or all of it. In this case, you could sell all of your holdings at the point marked by the down arrow.

Please note, the gap appeared after the entry which is a good thing, as it added momentum to the stock. If the trade went against the plan, you could have exited at the break of the trend line or the break of the support line at 59 approximately. Where to place stop loss, how to manage risk, how to manage trade, how to maximize profits and minimize losses are all yet to come. I want you to feel confident about the strategies discussed so far.

> **Actions To Take**
>
> 1. Pick a portfolio of stocks, check each stock and add pivot zones to the daily chart.
> 2. Identify Pivot level (P), Resistance levels R1, R2, Support levels S1 and S2 and see how price reacts at these levels and how price travels from Pivot P to R1 and S1, from S2 to S1 etc. Repeat this on the weekly charts for the stocks in your list.

Price Patterns

I have included price pattern in this book mainly because of its predictive value, precision , probability and because it will help you to find a price objective or targets to book profits either partial or in full. No doubt they require a bit of practice but it is worth it. This will not only tell you if the price is going to continue or reverse, but will also provide a way of estimating the possible targets. This increases the probability of capturing bigger moves without fear and worry. Price patterns are also indicative of the collective behavior of people, the participants. It presents an idea of what they are thinking, with regards to buying, selling or holding. Because you are interested in stacking the possibilities in your favor.

The collective behavior of price point perception matters.

When collective pattern is present, it repeats itself. Patterns give you a higher probability of success. While using price patterns to arrive at a price objective, always pay attention to volume; and how it is increasing and decreasing as price increases and decreases. This will help you to avoid mistakes in identifying the patterns correctly. If you are not interested in precision and are happy and contended with simple solution then either you can use Moving average crossovers or indicators or combination of both.

These when combined with volume, Gaps and trend lines, you get good results. But if you love precision trades then price patterns are a must have.

No method is one hundred percent perfect. That is why risk control is always required.

Continuation and Reversal of Price Patterns

There are two types of price pattern, continuation and reversal. A reversal pattern must have a prior trend. Top reversals are shorter in duration, quick and volatile. Bottom reversals take time and are generally smaller in range. Reversal pattern indicates that a major price reversal is in action. Continuous price patterns are intermediate in nature, and occur when the price tries to go sideways from the prevailing major trend. Continuous patterns appear to confirm that prices are about to continue in the direction of the trend, and therefore give an accurate price objective. (Use buy stop orders for trading continuation pattern instead of market order. Different order types will be explained in the Managing Trade chapter). You must remember that the price objectives given for each price pattern are the minimum target, and often the price gives you a lot more.

Major Continuation Patterns	Major Reversal Patterns
Flags and Pennants	V tops and V bottoms
Triangles (Ascending, Descending, Symmetrical and Expanding or Broadening formation)	Double tops and bottoms
Wedges (Raising and Falling)	Triple or Multiple tops and bottoms
Continuous Head and Shoulder	Head and shoulders
Trading range or Congestion or Rectangle	Rounding or sauce pattern

Fig 3.16.b Major Price Pattern Classification

Major Continuation Patterns

Continuation patterns indicate that price will continue in the direction of the primary trend, and also give us a target. Some of these patterns have a tendency to retrace before continuing, so it is important not to use a tight stop loss for these patterns. Flags and pennants normally form within 15 bars (15 days on a daily chart, 15 weeks on weekly chart, etc.), triangle patterns need at least 15 bars, and wedges extend for long periods of time. It is important to remember that some of these patterns could retrace before meeting the target. You should always try to enter on the break outside the pattern, using a buy stop order. (Buy stop order is discussed in the Trade Management section). Now, let's discuss the continuous patterns, starting with flags and pennants.

Flags and Pennants

Measure the distance from the bottom of the pole to the peak, where the flags or pennants formation started, and then add this to the breakout point to get the target (Fig 3.17). Volume should be light during the flag or pennant formation, but should still be higher before the start of the formation and later as it breaks out. Flag is like two parallel trend lines, but sloping in the opposite direction to the prevailing trend. Pennant is two trend lines converging horizontally. It looks like a symmetrical triangle, but generally lasts for less than fifteen days.

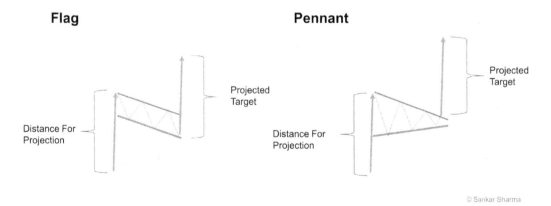

Fig 3.17 Flag and Pennant Pattern

Fig. 3.18 is an example of a UK stock in downtrend, in October 2015. As the price dropped to 17.7%, volume kept increasing. Then there is a rectangle pause period before the trade broke the trend line or the flag, denoted by two parallel lines. During the flag formation, comparable volume was declining as the price was increasing. As the downtrend continued, the volume picked up again. The vertical price drop measuring 17.7% is called Pole. The target measure is the same as 17.7%.

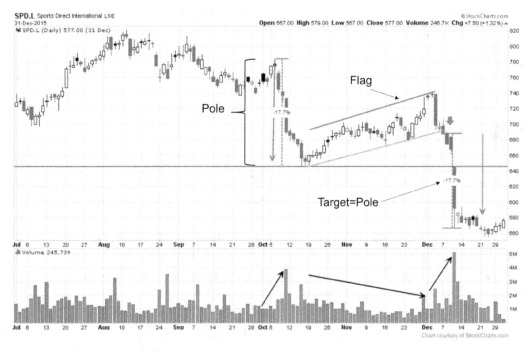

Fig 3.18 Flag Pattern –Sports Direct UK

Pennant Example

Fig. 3.19 is an example of pennant that formed repeatedly in one of the UK FTSE 100 stocks, Aberdeen Asset Management. It is important to note that most of these actually travel beyond the projected target. This is evident in Fig 3.19, where the projected target of 9.8% is met and the stock travelled beyond that. An example of price resolved to the downside. Fig 3.20, Amazon weekly chart, shows a pennant formation with 19.1% of the pole target met. This is a good example of where price resolved to the upside. Also it is important to note that since this is a continuation pattern, prices could go well beyond its recent highs.

Chapter 3: Strategies

Fig 3.19 Pennant Pattern – Aberdeen Asset Management UK

Fig 3.20 Pennant Pattern – Amazon

> **Actions To Take**
>
> 1. Flick through S&P 500 stocks or FTSE 250 or stocks from your local exchange and identify flags and pennants. If you can't find any at the first glance, it is likely that there aren't any. Do not be disappointed, and keep looking for the next price pattern.
> 2. If you find a pattern, draw them on the charts and save them for future use.
> 3. Draw projections and targets to see how they worked.
> 4. Repeat this exercise until you find a pattern.

Triangle Price patterns

This includes the ascending triangles (bullish), descending triangles (bearish) and symmetrical triangles illustrated in Fig 3.21. It is important to note that for all these patterns, you need at least three touches minimum on either side of the reversal points, and the price should not have gaps in-between the swings. The price should travel cleanly from one side to the other. You should look for prices that are hovering near the break point level in the final stages. For more aggressive entry, you can actually go intraday. For beginners, it is often better to wait until the price closes outside the triangle formation. The best way to trade using triangle pattern is by using buy stop order. Do not enter into the trade using market order. Measure the height of the widest part of the triangle, and project the distance from the breakout point. The volume should be increasing near the breakout and after. Pullbacks are often common with these patterns, and tight stops are unproductive. So you must use Risk Management Techniques.

Chapter 3: Strategies

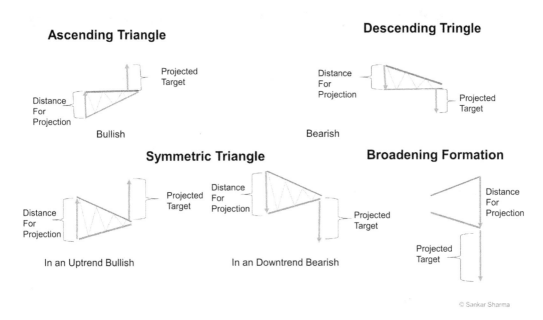

Fig 3.21 Ascending and Descending Pattern

Ascending triangle

An ascending triangle is normally bullish, and therefore you should expect the prior trend to be up. Ascending triangles can be identified by flat tops and raised bottoms. They should have at least two touches on the flat top, which indicates horizontal resistance. Important ascending triangles that form at the base of a chart near the bottom are often strong, and indicate long term trends. Typically, an ascending triangle requires at least 15 bars to form on the daily chart, or 15 bars (not etched on stone but a preference) on weekly i.e. at least 3 months.

Fig 3.22.a. chart of associated British foods shows an ascending triangle with a target of 8.7%.

Fig 3.22.a. Example of Ascending Pattern ABF.L

Fig 3.22.b. Microsoft chart shows an ascending triangle that formed at the bottom of the chart, which has the price ending in a strong uptrend. For a perfect ascending triangle, you want the price to oscillate smoothly from end to end between the walls. As the price drops within the pattern, you need volume dropping. Similarly you need volume to start picking up as price starts to raise and breakout. Fig 3.21 gives you details on how to measure the move for the target projection. If you can't spot the pattern properly on candlestick charts, try switching to a bar chart or line chart. Bar charts are normally preferred to line charts.

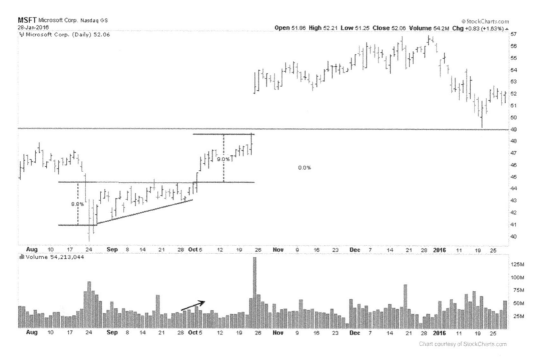

Fig 3.22.b. Example of Ascending Pattern Microsoft

Descending triangle

Descending triangles are bearish patterns. Prior to a descending triangle, you should often expect a downtrend in price. Descending triangle is identified by flat bottoms and falling tops. You should have at least two touches on the bottom and three touches on the falling tops. If you spot any gaps in the formation of the triangle, and the price fails to oscillate between the walls of the triangle, then it invalidates the pattern and you should avoid it. Fig 3.23 chart of Facebook shows a descending triangle. It is important to point out that a price pattern will only work if it is easy to spot. You should not be forcing it, or it will fail.

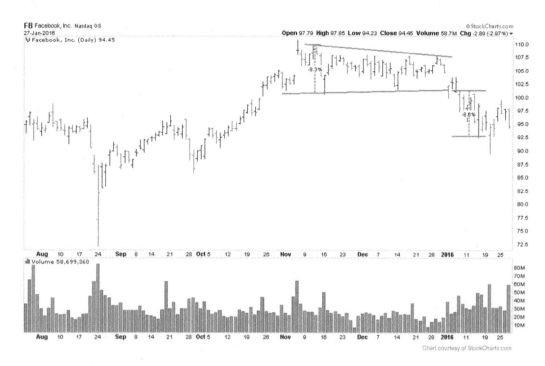

Fig 3.23 Example of Descending Pattern

It is important to note that patterns have their share of imperfections. It is not uncommon to see a triangle within triangle patterns. Once the objective price is getting closer, it is a good idea to tighten your stops close to that price.

Symmetrical triangle

The price generally breaks out of symmetrical triangles in the direction of the previous trend. In symmetrical triangles, you have one down trending trend line, one up trending trend line, and both will be converging in the right hand side of the chart before breakout. If the price is in a downtrend and a symmetrical triangle formation appears, on breakout, the price will continue to be bearish. Similarly, if the price is in an uptrend and you get a symmetrical triangle, expect the price to break out to the upside. Fig 3.24.a. Oracle chart shows the symmetrical pattern.

Fig 3.21 gives you details on how to measure the move for the target projection for a symmetrical triangle pattern.

Fig 3.24.a. Example of Symmetrical Pattern

Certain investors express doubt on whether price patterns exist in an initial placement (IPO) stock, and whether they would work if they did exist. Fig 3.24.b. chart of a 2015 IPO shows a pennant and a symmetrical pattern, and both met the targets perfectly. For target measures, refer to Fig 3.21.

Fig 3.24.b Examples of Price patterns in recent IPO stock

Fig 3.25 and Fig 3.26 is an example of a PayPal chart. Notice how you could have drawn the symmetrical lines in two different ways, each with different profit targets. Which one would you choose and why? Choose the one that has (a) clean movement between the walls of the pattern and (b) choose the conservative profit projection as a target if in doubt.

Fig 3.25. Example of incorrectly drawn pattern with least touches

Chapter 3: Strategies

Fig 3.26 Example of correctly drawn pattern lines with correct touches

Actions To Take
1. Flick through S&P 500 stocks or FTSE 250 or stocks from your local exchange and identify ascending, descending and symmetrical triangle patterns. If you can't find any at the first glance, it is likely that there aren't any.
2. If you find a pattern, draw them on the charts and save them for future use.
3. Draw projections and targets to see how they worked.
4. Repeat this exercise until you find a pattern.

Wedges

There are two types of wedges. Rising wedges are considered bearish and both of their trend lines slope upwards. Falling wedges are considered bullish. For falling wedges, both trend lines slope downwards. You need at least 3 touches on one side and 2 touches on the opposite side. Entry is after the stop closes outside the pattern. Target generally is at the beginning of the wedge.

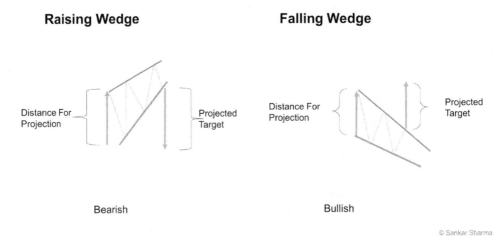

Fig 3.27 Raising and Falling Wedge

Charts of Jd.com (Fig 3.28) and Adobe systems (Fig 3.29) give examples of the raising wedge. The raising wedge is bearish. On the contrary, the falling wedge is bullish. Refer to Fig 3.27 for target projection measures.

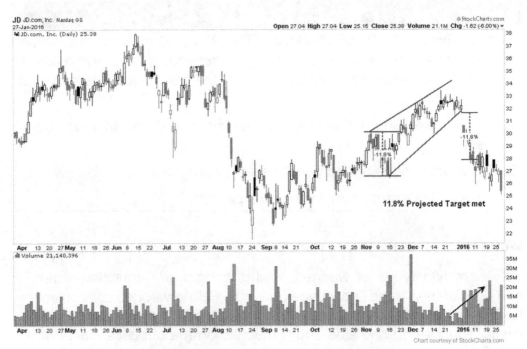

Fig 3.28 Example 01 of Raising Wedge

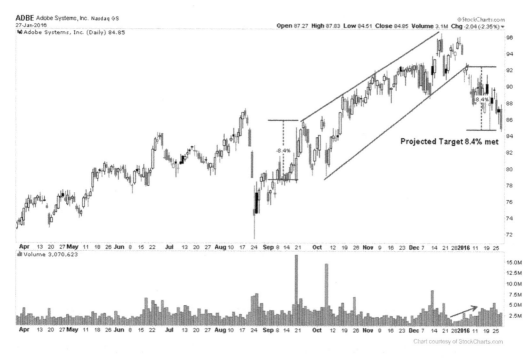

Fig 3.29 Example 02 of Raising Wedge

Inverse Head and Shoulders

Before entering the trade, wait for the price to close above the two peaks that make up the neck line. Measure the distance from the bottom of the head to the neckline, and add this to the breakout point to get the target. Inverse head and shoulders is a continuous price pattern, and is also known as a continuous head and shoulders pattern.

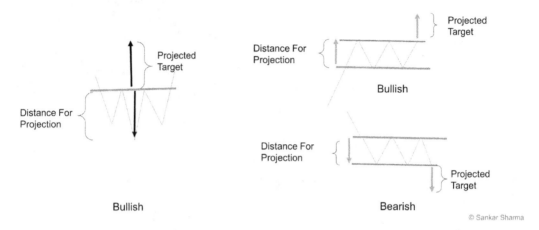

Fig 3.30 Inverse Head and Shoulders and Rectangular Pattern

Fig 3.31 shows an example of Inverse head and shoulders, a continuation pattern. The projected target was 16.4%, which was comfortably met. Fig 3.30 shows how to measure the move for the target projection.

Trading range, congestion or rectangle

The trading range, range, congestion or rectangle pattern (Fig 3.32. Cisco chart for example) is one of the common patterns used by many traders. It is often easy to spot. It is important to note that if you trade within the range, then an investor will end up losing money. On the contrary, if you trade on the range breakout of it as a continuous pattern, the probability of success is high. Range is normally identified by drawing a rectangle as shown in the Fig.3.32.

Beginners should concentrate on one pattern, master it and then move to the next. The best way to be good at this is by dedicating more screen time to spotting price patterns.

Chapter 3: Strategies

Fig 3.31 Example Inverse Head and shoulders INTC

Fig 3.32 Example of Range, Rectangle, Congestion or Coil Breakout

Fig 3.32 shows the rectangular pattern breakout to the down side and the target achievement of 6.5%. Refer to Fig 3.30 for details on how to measure the targets.

> **Actions To Take**
>
> 1. Flick through S&P 500 stocks, FTSE 250 or stocks from your local exchange and identify Inverse head and shoulders and triangular patterns. If you can't find any at the first glance, it is likely that there aren't any. Do not force a pattern for the sake of it.
> 2. If you find a pattern, draw them on the charts and save them for future use.
> 3. Draw projections and targets to see how they worked.
> 4. Repeat this exercise until you find a pattern.

Reversal Patterns

The best place to use reversal patterns is at market tops and market bottom. Always use confluence and volume for increasing the probability of success. Let me recap the reversal patterns.

Major Reversal Patterns
V tops and V bottoms
Double tops and bottoms
Triple or multiple tops and bottoms
Head and shoulders
Rounding or sauce pattern

Fig 3.33.a. Major Reversal Patterns

Chapter 3: Strategies

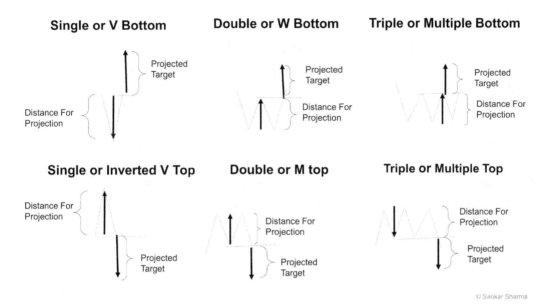

Fig 3.33.b. Major Reversal Patterns

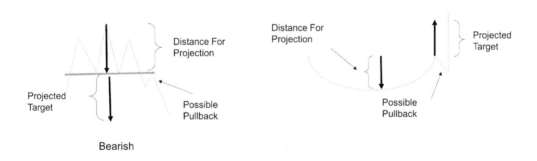

Fig 3.33.c. Major Reversal Patterns

Single Bottom

Single bottom recovery is often known as V type recovery. This is generally rare, but for a confirmed V shaped recovery, the recovery must be fierce and strong in the upward direction. As the price starts to break out after the V shape reversal, volume must increase along with the price movement. Some investors are comfortable with the candlestick pattern and some are comfortable with bar charts. For this reason, you will find both types of charts in the book. In the case of the stock Activision (ATVI) Fig 3.34a, a price reached the target at a slow pace, whereas in the case of the stock Dollar Tree (DLTR) Fig 3.34b, the price reached its destination fairly quickly.

Fig 3.34.a. Example of V Bottom Reversal ATVI

Chapter 3: Strategies

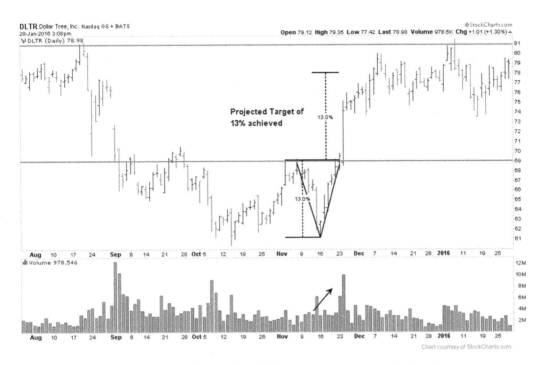

Fig 3.34.b. Example of V Bottom Reversal DLTR

Double Bottom

For valid double bottom, you must wait for the price to close above the peak in the middle. The stop loss in this case would be a few points below the previous trough. Fig 3.35, Weekly chart of SLAB, shows the strength of W pattern reversal and target met comfortably.

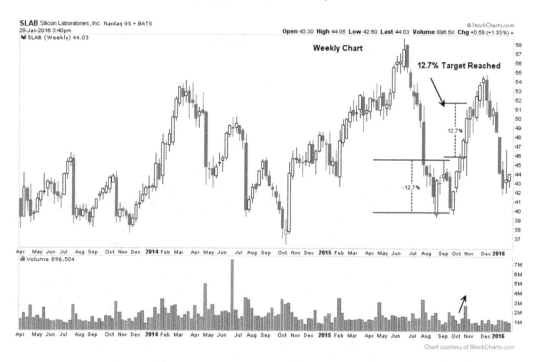

Fig 3.35 Example of Double Bottom Reversal SLAB

Triple or Multiple bottom

Triple or multiple bottom pattern is much stronger than double and V bottom. Normally, a stock that breaks out of triple bottom often pulls back before it proceeds in the direction of the break. Fig 3.36 Domino's pizza UK (DOM.L) stock shows triple bottom, a strong reversal and a price which meets the target and beyond.

Fig 3.36 Example of Triple or Multiple Bottom Reversal DOM.L

Single Top

Similar to single bottom, this is not reliable unless the reaction is fierce and fast. So avoid single tops when possible. If you refer to Fig 3.37 Baxter (BAX), you will see that the price is reversed at a very high volume, which is probably a result of poor earnings or bad news. Notice the retracement. This often happens with price patterns, which is something to bear in mind while placing stops.

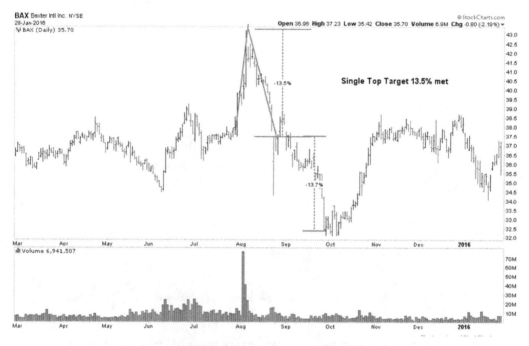

Fig 3.37 Example of Single Top BAX

Chapter 3: Strategies

Double Top

This is a quite commonly traded pattern and is often referred to as M for murder, it appears at the market tops. In the event of double top, the entry point comes when the price closes below the bottom, between the two peaks. You cannot use tight stop losses because there will always be pull back that you need to watch out for. The first target is the distance from one peak, to the low of the bottom, in the middle of the two peaks. Fig 3.38 Stock General Motors (GM) shows the projected target measure from B to C. The valley in the center of the M shape – 3.9% – was met to the downside.

Fig 3.38 Example of Double Top GM

Triple or Multiple Top

Similar to double top, enter on the close below the bottoms among the three peaks. Measure the distance from the smallest peak to the bottom of three or more peaks, and add this to the close price of the break point to get the target. Fig 3.39 shows multiple tops in Intel Corp. (INTC). This shows a very strong reversal signal, and results in two price gaps and accelerated downside price movement. The projected target at 4.5% is comfortably met.

Fig 3.39 Example of Triple or Multiple Top INTC

Head and Shoulder Top

As a beginner, you should only trade horizontal head and shoulders. Reversal patterns in general require a lot of practice and research into several hundred charts. When price breaks below the neck line, enter the trade and measure the distance from the peak of the head to the neckline. Then, add this to the break point closing price, to get the target. Fig 3.40, chart of Kroger Co, shows a clear head and shoulders reversal pattern.

Fig 3.40 Example of Reverse Head and Shoulders Reversal KR

Cup and Handle

Cup and Handle is another reverse pattern. In the case of cup and handle pattern, the target price is the depth of the cup. As the pattern has a tendency to pull back first, it is called a handle. But for this reason, some beginners may find it bit difficult to trade.

Actions To Take

1. Flick through S&P 500 stocks or FTSE 250 or stocks from your local exchange and look for reversal patterns. If you can't find any at the first glance, it is likely that there aren't any.

2. From the list of patterns, see if you can spot two of your favorites and master them before you move onto others. Don't forget about trend lines, support and resistance, pivots and Fibonacci.

Volume

Beginners in the stock market must always use volume in addition to price. Volume gives a very good indication about the liquidity of the stock. Stock with trading volume in millions compared to stock with trading volume in thousands has high liquidity, and is therefore much safer. It is better to avoid stocks that has 'Trading volumes' in thousands. While you might be able to buy this stock easily, you will struggle to sell it without losing a lot of money, due to poor liquidity. There are some sceptics who do not wish to use volume in their investing or trading. As a result, they lose out on some good opportunities or lose money on their investments. Never undermine Trading volume.

Fig 3.41, Provident Financial stock listed on the London Stock Exchange, shows a volume spike on 30th November 2015, in what appears to be sell volume. If you happened to own this stock at that time, you could have kept tight stops, sold the stock in the following days and saved yourself a 21.7% loss, provided you gave consideration to volume and noted the volume spike and price stalling. Always use volume in conjunction with price and not in isolation.

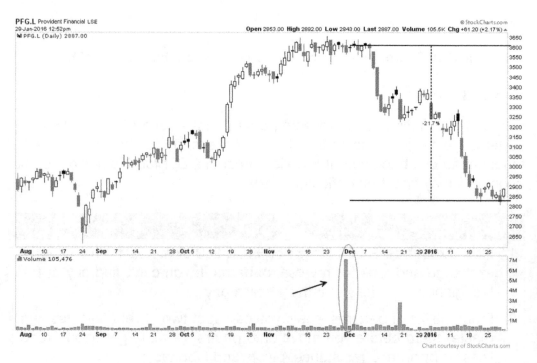

Fig 3.41 Sell Volume Impact PFG.L

Moving averages

Moving averages are available as an indicator to plot on your charts. Simple moving average shorts are referred to as SMA, and exponential moving average as EMA. 10-day SMA based on closing has an average of 10 days' closing price. Exponential moving average gives importance to recent prices. 10, 20, 50, 100, 200 and multiples of 100 are used most commonly as support and resistance or cross overs for buy and sell. Some use EMAs and others SMAs. Some use Fibonacci series or moving averages like 3,5,8,13,21,34,55,89,144 etc. You often hear people say that the stock looks bullish, as it is above 50 EMA or 200 EMA and bearish because the price is below 50 or 200 EMA. In other words, if the price is below 50 EMA, it implies that the price is heading down and vice versa. This can be used as a form of trend filter for stocks. It acts as a quick visual tool, but one must remember that this is a derivative of price. So far all of the things I discussed prior to the moving averages are purely based on price and volume. I have included moving averages for completion here.

Fig 3.42a is an example chart of Chipotle (CMG) that combines moving averages 10EMA, 20 EMA and reversal candlestick pattern (Evening Star and Bearish Engulfing candlestick patterns). The bearish candlestick patterns help you to confirm the price reversals from up trend to down. For confluence – volume, support and resistance levels can be used. This nicely leads us to the next topic the profitable candlestick patterns.

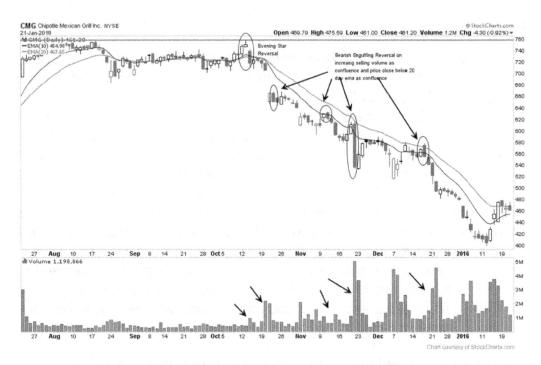

Fig 3.42 a Major Reversal Candlestick patterns and Moving Averages

Actions To Take
1. Go to S&P 500 or FTSE 350 (FTSE100 & FTSE 250) daily stocks. Add a 50 day simple moving average (SMA), 200-day SMA.
2. Mark the stocks as 'bearish' when 50-Day SMA cross 200-Day SMA to the 'down side', and 'bullish' when you see that the 50-Day SMA is crossing the 200-Day SMA to the upside
3. Search for IBB Biotech iShares, add 50-day SMA, 200-day SMA, and 500-day SMA. Examine how these averages act as support and resistance on the daily and weekly charts.

Profitable Candlestick Patterns

In this section, the discussion is focused only on reversal candlestick patterns that are often found at resistance, support levels or market tops and bottoms. These must not be used in isolation. They can be used as another tool for confluence, in the same way that volume is used for confluence as discussed in the earlier section on price patterns.

Fig 3.42b Major Bullish and Bearish Reversal Candlestick Patterns

Bullish Reversal Candlestick Patterns	Bearish Reversal Candlestick patterns
Bullish Doji Star	Bearish Doji Star
Southern Doji	Northern Doji
Dragon Fly	Gravestone Doji
Hammer	Inverted Hammer
Bullish Engulfing	Bearish Engulfing
Bullish Kicker	Bearish Kicker
Morning Star	Evening Star

The candlestick patterns mentioned in Fig 3.42b are not an exhaustive list, but you will notice that some of the patterns frequently appear in the market. Do not use them in isolation for your investment decisions, and always use them for confluence. While using the candlesticks, it is really important to take into account the previous price movement and price trend, represented as small vertical lines in Fig 3.43. The figure gives a summary of all Reversal Candlestick Patterns both for Bullish (Reversal to upside) and Bearish patterns. Do not make decisions based on one candle alone.

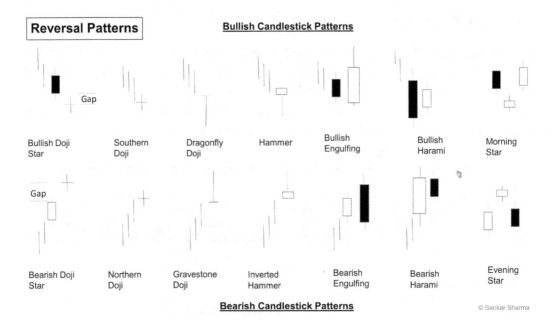

Fig 3.43 Reversal Candlestick patterns

The trick with candlestick pattern is to be able to distinguish between bullish and bearish reversal patterns. Most importantly, it is essential to recognize the look of the pattern itself. Bullish reversal pattern indicates price is going to turn to the upside and Bearish reversal pattern indicates price is going to turn to the downside.

In a Trading session, if the open price and the closing price are the same, then it is a 'Doji' formation. A 'doji star' is formed when there is gap between the prior price falling (candle filled, colored red or black) or falling price (empty candle, colored white). A 'dragonfly doji' is a doji with a long, lower shadow. The open, high, and close prices are at the session's high. The opposite of this is called gravestone doji. 'Northern doji' are doji that appear during a rally and southern doji are doji that appear during declines.

A 'bullish engulfing' pattern is comprised of a large white body that engulfs a small black body in a downtrend. A 'bearish engulfing 'pattern occurs when selling pressure overwhelms buying force, as reflected by a long black body engulfing a small white body in an uptrend. An 'evening star' is a top reversal pattern formed by three candles. If a small white body candle forms and gaps, immediately succeeding this is a black body candle that closes into the first large white candle. This pattern is called evening star. Opposite of this is the morning star pattern. Harami is a two candlestick pattern in which the small body holds within the prior session's unusually large body, and is opposite in color to the first one. 'Harami' implies that the previous trend is concluded, and that bulls and bears are in truce. There are a lot of variations available for interpretation but the ones mentioned here should be more than enough to serve you well, if applied appropriately. Biggest mistake many make with candlestick is that they make decisions based on a single candle. If you do that, it is a sure way to lose money.

Let me share with you, how to use these patterns and the rules that goes with it.

Case study 1: Pattern: Evening Star –Type: Bearish Pattern

Where to use?

You see this pattern at Resistance points, near down trend lines, Resistance R1 or Resistance R2 or Resistance R3 levels of pivot lines or near Major Moving Averages like 200 Day or 50 Day. This candlestick pattern works like a magic.

Ref. picture 3.43.a- Freeport-McMoRan -FCX between 2015-Oct and 2016-March. Please pay attention to point B.

1. You draw a Trend Line between point 1 and point 2

2. Draw a Parallel channel trend line to touch point A. Why? Because at this point, you don't know about point B yet. You just have Point A

3. Now the question is what happens at point B? Can you sell here? It is called shorting i.e. selling first and buying later.

At Point, B you have the Peak or Top, with three candles giving you the 'Evening Star' formation. Is this near Trend line resistance? Yes. Is 'Evening star' a bearish formation? Yes. Would you Buy or sell at Point B? Of course sell. Before point B is the trend up? Yes, secondary small up trend in Primary down Trend. Where is the Entry? You enter below the low of the day on the 3rd candle of the Bearish Evening star formation. You are selling the stock first and buying later (This is called shorting). Marked by horizontal line at point C. Target is the bottom of the Trend line support, Point D in the chart. The trade is complete.

Also, if you are familiar with option, you could have benefited from this trade. These candlestick patterns are called reversal pattern because they indicate price is going to reverse. The immediate previous trend, in this case, the 'bearish candlestick pattern' reversed immediate to secondary short term up trend at point B. Good simple trade. Note, you have not used any indicators for your decisions.

Can you spot a Morning Star Reversal pattern in this chart? If not, see the next Case study example.

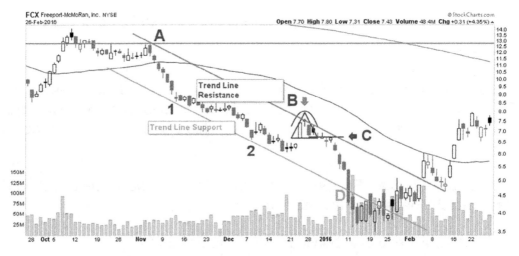

Fig 3.43.a. Evening Star Bearish Pattern Case Study

Case study 2: Pattern: Morning Star –Type: Bullish Pattern

Focus on point E. (Ref. picture 3.43.b). You have a Morning star formation (Reversal Bullish pattern, meaning you expect the next move to the upside). This Morning star obeyed the rules. It's formed near the 50-Day Moving Average. Entry point is above the high of third candle of the morning star candlestick pattern. (When buying you want to buy high of the third candle and while selling the low of the third candle). At point E, you have a trough or valley. Valley formed after price made a higher high and lower low (not marked on the chart to avoid overcrowding of notes). Entry is at point F and

Target is previous resistance zone drawn through point B. That makes point G as a potential Target. Note between point E and F the increase in volume.

Note at Point G (Ref 3.43.b), you have another morning star. But your trade never triggered because your entry is above the high of the third candle at G. There is no new candle formed after that to the upside and you have no trade.

Fig 3.43.b. Morning star -Reversal Bullish Pattern Case Study

Case Study 3: Bullish Morning Star Candlestick with Price Pattern

Here is another example, JC Penny (JCP). In this case, you do your Candlestick analysis and to that you add the price pattern. See the result. Ref. Fig 3.43.c where the Morning star pattern near the 50-day moving average is shown. You have the usual rules obeyed nicely. You have Morning star near the 50-Day Moving Average (For 50-day and 200-Day Moving average, simple moving averages are always used. For lower moving averages use Exponential). You have a trend line support, a bullish doji formed which also happens to be the first Higher Low on 50-day moving average. No higher high yet. When the morning star formed, you have a new Higher Low. You have a trough. Volume increased when morning star was formed. Your Entry order is above the high of the Morning star 3rd candle. At this point, no price pattern is added. (Ref Fig 3.43.c. Morning star -Reversal Bullish Pattern without Price Pattern).

Fig 3.43.c. Morning star -Reversal Bullish Pattern without Price Pattern

Fig 3.43.d. Morning star -Reversal Bullish Pattern with Price Pattern

If you refer to Fig 3.43.d ascending triangle price pattern was added. As soon as you add the price pattern, you now have the target at $10.25 staring at you. You can see how when you add these studies one at a time they clarify the trade with regards to where to enter, exit and place stop. Stop loss in this case will be below the trough of morning star pattern formation, immediately below the trend line.

To summarize, a beginner investor is better off mastering one bullish and bearish pattern before mastering the next. You may want to start with

Morning star and evening star or bullish and bearish engulfing (Ref 3.41) candlestick pattern to begin with.

Actions To Take
1. Go to your portfolio of stocks. For each chart, identify increasing volume zones and see how the price reacted to buy or sell.
2. Circle candlestick patterns at key support and resistance, trend lines, Fibonacci levels and pivot levels to see how the price reacted.
3. As with patterns, identify your favorite candlestick patterns to use as a confluence. Most people like doji and engulfing, but some prefer to trade with bull, bear or harami.

CHAPTER 4

SHORTLISTING STOCKS

Shortlisting stocks is a cherry picking process. You need to pick quality stocks from the universe of stock indices for analysis, for validating trend, identifying patterns and looking for confluence in order to stack probabilities in your favor. No doubt, when you first start, this will be a little challenging and sometimes a little frustrating. But, once you do it a few times with discipline, then it becomes as easy as brushing your teeth.

The first thing you need to decide upon is your trading time frame.

If you are investing for your child, you may be looking at a 5 to 10 year horizon. For pension accounts, you may be thinking of dividend paying stocks, if you are older and more aggressive momentum stocks (which hold for a maximum of 3 months), if you are much younger.

Imagine you are in the UK and want to pick one FTSE 100 and one FTSE 250 stock from the universe of 350 stocks, made up from FTSE 100 and FTSE 250 indices. Somebody in the US might be thinking of shortlisting one technology stock from NASDAQ 100 index, one DOW JONE 30 stock and one SMP 500 Stock. Now, this means selecting three stocks out of the total universe of several hundred stocks. The problem is that this might take a lot of time, possibly even a week or even more, to review and shortlist the stocks. Ideally, this should not take you more than 30 minutes. To achieve this feat, you need to use the charting software as discussed in the earlier chapters, and use the filter, scan or data mining criteria. All these words essentially mean the same thing.

For a beginner, it is very important that you keep your trading simple and do not over complicate things.

If you have a tendency to go after every new strategy or new indicator, or buy every software package available in the market, then it is likely you'll be making big mistakes. There are several ways you can pick stocks for pre-trade analysis. Once you filter them, you can store them in a list. This list is known as a watch list. These terms change based on the software provider.

Chapter 4: Shortlisting Stocks 93

Some of the easy ways to pick stocks for 'pre-trade analysis' are as follows:

1. A stock you read about in the papers, or heard about on the news.
2. By using search criteria (screener, filter, data mining all mean the same).
3. By doing sector analysis.
4. By doing top down analysis.
5. By picking stocks during earning season (avoid those whose earnings are due before you buy)
6. By new highs or new lows, top gainers or top losers, gap ups or gap downs.
7. Scanning stocks for price patterns and candlestick patterns.
8. By scanning for indicator crossover, like moving average crossovers etc. Most charting software provides the stock filtering as part of their service. You need a service that provides an end of day data service.

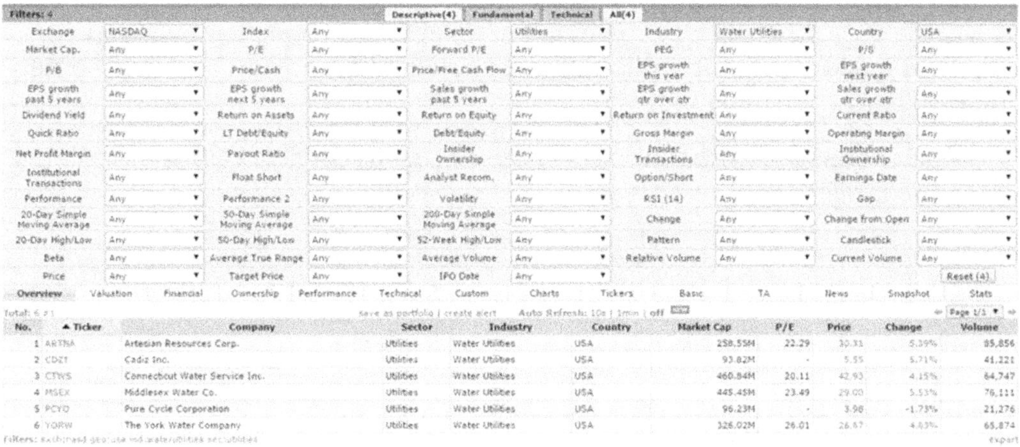

Fig 4.1 Example Screener

A screener is a great tool to help you find potential stocks. Some of the inputs, before you run this screener, come from completing pre-trade analysis.

Actions To Take

1. Pick one stock for each of the categories below:
   - A stock you have heard about or seen in the financial press or media.
   - A stock found by using search criteria in your charting software (screener, filter, data mining all mean the same).
   - By doing sector analysis.
   - By doing top down analysis.
   - Based on recent quarterly announcements in the USA (after earnings announcement).
   - From the top gainers list.
   - One gap up stock.
   - By scanning for price patterns.
   - Showing reversal candlestick patterns.
   - By scanning for indicator crossover like moving average cross overs
2. Add these to a spreadsheet ready for pre-trade analysis, and call this a 'watch list'.

CHAPTER 5

PRE-TRADE ANALYSIS

Once you have your watch list, with the list of candidates to invest or trade, it is mandatory to take each stock in your list and run it past a series of validity tests before committing your money. This is where pre-trade analysis comes into the picture.

The aim of pre-trade analysis is (a) to eliminate any unwelcome surprises, which could later prove to be costly and (b) to separate Good from bad and the ugly. There are two parts to this. First part is to do pre-trade analysis for a share you are thinking of purchasing. This has to be done prior to purchase of the stock. The second part is to do with the pre-trade analysis of the markets. This you will do when you are unsure of the market conditions. Markets never go up or down in a straight line. So when there are big fall in the market, you can make use of this analysis to protect your investments or to buy stocks cheap and benefit from it in the long run.

Example of an unwelcome surprise for a stock could be that there may be an earnings announcement due in 2 days' time. If you buy a stock prior to that, and then the company comes in with bad news, the analysts will start to downgrade the stocks and you'll be accumulating quick losses. I will discuss this further in the later part of the chapter.

What you see is not real, what you hear is not real. What you research and analyse is real.

CASE STUDY: Pre-Trade analysis for Validation

Below is a case study with a clear example of how I conducted my Pre-trade Analysis in Feb 2016 and benefitted from it.

The markets were falling since Jan 16, due to concerns on China's growth and the pace was picking up. On the media, there were talk of 'recession', but it is always important to validate the information you hear or see. Pre-trade analysis of the markets is part of this validation. You may appreciate its significance once you look back. You do Pre-trade analysis for the markets when necessary or in doubt. Whereas for a stock you do before purchase.

When I finished the Global Market SWOT analysis in Feb 2016, it quickly became apparent that there was only less than 30% chance of recession implying that the drop in Markets were merely a short term dip (pull back) and presenting good buying opportunity. It took me 20 min to collate the data for this and 10 min to conclude. I am sharing the exact steps I used for your benefit. Irrespective of the year, the steps for analysis are the same.

PART 1 - Pre-trade Market Analysis Feb 2016 -Checking the Markets and Market SWOT

Steps involved are

1. Check Market indices, Internals and market breadth. Check state of Dollar, Gold and Oil, Check Treasuries
2. Do Global SWOT analysis
3. Do Economy review – Use Unemployment, Growth, Customer spending Interest rates, Wage growth
4. Conduct sector analysis to validate

Each of these studies will help you to cross validate your inferences. I have used Technical analysis components that was discussed in the last chapter, for analyzing the charts. In this chapter, you will notice data for several countries around the globe are shown but US will be the primary focus.

I used S&P, Dow Jones, NASDAQ composite, NYSE and Russel as examples in this book. You should check market breadth, i.e. how many stocks are advancing and how many are declining? What is the volume like? Do a sector analysis review, and check to see if money is going from one sector to another on a weekly, monthly and quarterly basis, depending on your investing period. Avoid picking stocks based only on daily sector rotation, because on a down or totally bullish day, you will have all sectors in red or green respectively. You should stick to monthly and quarterly charts if your holding period is for a few months only.

A quick note on sector analysis. Stocks are grouped into industry and industries are grouped into sectors, while sectors are affected by economic cycles. As the economy expands and contracts, certain sectors will be more in favor and some out of favor. At present, the US markets have a major influence on global markets, so it made sense to use them in my analysis.

Before you start your analysis, arrange your charts in the following order:

1. US market indices and market indices of your country (Fig 5.1).
2. Market breadth charts, advance and decliners, volume of advance and decliners, and highs and lows (Fig 5.2).
3. Treasuries (Fig 5.3).
4. Volatility index, gold, silver, oil and dollar charts (Fig 5.4).

Market Indices SWOT

Market indices SWOT involves identifying strength, weakness, opportunities and threats relating to the market. It is important that all market participants follow this routine. Before you start, it is a good idea to add a 20-day exponential (EMA) and 50-day simple moving average (SMA) to your charts. For the purpose of interpretation, if the stock is above 50-day SMA, then mark the chart as bullish. If the stock is below this, mark it as bearish. If your investing time period is beyond a year, it is worth using 200-day SMA. Again, you should price anything above this as bullish, and anything below it as bearish. If you have a mid or short-term period as your time horizon, and the 20-day SMA is above 50, you can say the chart is bullish. Likewise, you can say the chart is bearish, if the 20-day SMA crossed below 50. This applies to all of the charts discussed in this section. Some professionals don't even touch a stock whose price is below the 50-day simple moving average.

Next, add support, resistance and trend lines. You will be amazed by the clarity this presents at the end of the analysis. If you are using stockcharts.com for checking the indices, then you need to note that ticker symbols for these are prefixed with $.(Ref Fig.5.1 for the list of U.S indices in question and how the ticker symbols are prefixed with the dollar sign, notation followed by stockcharts.com).

Chapter 5: Pre-Trade Analysis

CandleGlance: $SPX, $INDU, $COMPQ, $NYA, $RUT

Simple Moving Averages: 20-period 50-period

Fig 5.1 US Stock Market Indices

Incidentally, all of the resistance, support lines, trend lines and moving averages are part of maintaining a journal for future reference. Once they are drawn, you only need to amend it if any of the trends change.

If the 20-day simple moving average (colored blue) is above 50-day Simple moving average (colored red), you can mark bullish in the table. If 50-day SMA is above 20-day SMA, you can mark it as bearish. If the price is in-between the averages, you can mark it too for confirmation. You can then see overall, if the markets are in synchronization or deviating from each other (e.g. Russell small cap diverging from S&P and Dow big caps). Moving averages are lagging indicators of price, but they could act as a good guide for visual interpretation of trends.(If prices are making higher highs and lower lows then the charts are in an uptrend, if the prices are making lower lows and lower highs, the charts are in a downtrend).

From the charts in (Fig. 5.1), it is clear that all the US indices S&P 500($SPX), Dow Jones industrial average ($INDU), NASDAQ ($COMPQ), NYSE Index ($NYA) and Russell 2000 Index ($RUT) are in bear territory (falling in price and in a down trend).

The next step in Market Indices SWOT Analysis is to check Market Breadth for U.S. Fig 5.2 shows the advance and decliners ($NYAD), volume of advance and decliners ($NYUD), and highs and lows ($NYHL). These are for NYSE. The same US market breadth indicators were also checked for Amex and NASDAQ markets. You can see a common theme with new lows and weaknesses everywhere in U.S related indices.

Fig 5.2 Market Breadth

Now how can you benefit from these charts (without even looking at a detailed chart for each of these). If you had U.S stocks that made you money, you could have tightened your stops or got out when (Fig. 5.1) Dow crossed down below 17000, or S&P crossed down the 2000 mark. If there are any bounces in these indices, 17000 on the Dow and 2000 on the S&P, they are going to act as initial resistance.

You may want to take note that round numbers generally act as good support or resistance.

Many traders see the round numbers as psychological levels in the market. Secondly, if you are an advanced trader, you could have either taken short position (selling first and buying back later to make money) or used options for hedging or traded Inverse ETFs. Finally, you would not have bought any new U.S shares, thus avoiding quick sinking losses in your portfolio.

Next, let us examine U.S treasuries in Fig 5.3. 10 Year ($TNX), 5 Year ($FVX), 3 Month ($IRX) and 30 Year ($TYX). These charts have 20-Day Simple Moving Average (coloured Blue) and 50-Day Simple moving average (coloured red). You can already see that while stocks rallied in October 2015, the treasuries rallied in November 2015. The data is as of February 2016.

Fig 5.3 Treasuries

If you examine (Fig. 5.4) US markets Volatility index ($VIX - represents fear or greed in the markets), gold ($XAU), oil ($OSX) and U.S Dollar ($USD) it gives us quite a valuable insight. We can see that people are not rushing to gold. Gold is often used as a safe haven during recession. Oil prices are continuing to drop. Now, take a look at dollar. Dollar has been rising steadily. This means that US exports might slow over a period, as the other countries with falling currencies will have difficulty in buying U.S products, if U.S is exporting to them. This could dent the earnings of US companies, producing goods or services in U.S and solely rely on revenue from external markets.

CandleGlance: $VIX, $XAU, $OSX, $USD

Simple Moving Averages: 20-period 50-period

Fig 5.4 Volatility Index, Gold, Silver, Oil and Dollar

So how can you, the investor, benefit from raising dollar? If you are living in a country where the country's currency is weak against the dollar, you could have easily opened a dollar account and put your savings there. With the dollar appreciating, and with the interest rate hikes etc., you could have a low-risk high-reward return scenario. This is not investment advice, but this information is powerful if you put it to use.

Fig. 5.5.a lists the dollar cross country rates against other countries as on January 2016. It shows (Fig.5.5.a) how other currencies performed and how it affected the exchange rates in UK, India, China, Canada or South Africa etc. Of course people in U.S could take advantage of their strong currency and travel to a country of weak currency or buy property there with long term view. For example you can see Peso fell 57.2% against dollar between Feb 2015 and Jan 2016.

NAME	1-YEAR Percent Change compared to USD (Feb 2015 Jan 2016)
U.S. Dollar/Argentine Peso	57.02%
U.S. Dollar/Russian Ruble	21.31%
U.S. Dollar/South African Rand	44.34%
U.S. Dollar/Canadian Dollar	19.32%
U.S. Dollar/Mexican Peso	22.54%
U.S. Dollar/British Pound	5.00%
U.S. Dollar/Euro FX	8.56%
U.S. Dollar/Australian Dollar	16.83%
U.S. Dollar/Chinese Yuan	6.09%

Jan 2016 Courtesy © Barchart.com

Fig 5.5.a Performance of Major countries currency against strong US Dollar

In Feb 2016, let us see how low oil and commodities are impacting upon the currencies of other countries. Canada, Russia, Australia, South Africa and Mexico to name a few were all affected, and their currencies (Fig 5.5.a) were low against the strong US dollar. This means that shorting these currencies could yield good returns against the US dollar. On the other hand, as interest rates starts increasing, dollar rate increases. Falling commodity and oil prices affects countries like Canada, Russia, Venezuela and other producers of the commodities and oil.

Fig 5.5b. shows the Global Short Term (1 to 2 years) SWOT analysis, Strength, Weakness, Opportunities and Threats.

Purpose of this analysis is to see if any of the findings are validating the 'recession' concerns as of Feb 2016. Looking at the table one can see that U.S Dollar is strong and impacting other countries. Commodity and oil have fallen considerably. Low oil price had an impact on oil producing countries like Venezuela. Brexit, US and Europe election could cause headwinds but may not warrant a recession in 2016. Global growth slowed around the world but no serious concerns or contagion risks were found as part of the analysis (Ref 5.5.b). SWOT analysis implied that the recent fall in the markets was just a big pull back and presented buying opportunity.

Economy Review

The purpose of this section is to give you a general overview of economy related terms, to accelerate your learning and at the same time to cross check if there were recession fears to worry about or whether the scenario in Feb 2016 was just a short term pull back. When recession hits, some worry about their employment, whereas the informed investor sees opportunities to pick stocks at beaten down prices.

In this section, I'll talk about various Economic indicators. Generally economic indicators even though lagging indicators, provides you enough answers to the question in focus.

Strength	Weakness	Opportunities	Threats
Dollar	Oil price fallen below thirty dollars.	Dollar Raising.	Sovereign risk. Countries holding high level of debt, countries that produce oil and commodities are experiencing growth issues.
	US indices are showing weakness	US Elections might present some new opportunities	Brexit vote, US Elections and Italy Elections could produce volatility in the markets.
	Commodity prices and energy prices falling. Steel industry is under stress.		Low commodity prices indicate lack of demand.

Strength	Weakness	Opportunities	Threats
	Bond yields not looking attractive.		World economies are showing signs of weakness.
	China markets showing major weakness.	May present opportunities in energy companies	Oil is down but Dow transport index is also showing weakness.
	Global economies looking weak, and growth is showing weakness.		Currencies getting devalued in certain parts of the world.

© Sankar Sharma

Fig 5.5.b Global SWOT Analysis

U.S Consumer price index (CPI) Fig 5.6 indicates price level of goods and services purchased by households. It showed it moved from negative in Dec 2015 to Positive in 2016. So, not validating any recession fears.

CPI Growth	First Quarter 2016	Last Quarter 2015
United States CPI Growth	0.20%	-0.20%
Canada inflation/Growth	1.40%	1.00%
Eurozone HICP Growth	0.20%	0.20%
UK CPI Growth	0.10%	0.10%

Key for all the tables listed below: Current =2016 and 3Months Ago= Last quarter 2015   Data Curtesy © Barchart.com

Fig 5.6 CPI Growth

Unemployment rate (Fig. 5.7), showed that U.S Unemployment was at historically low levels and it was nowhere near the recessionary levels of 2008- 2009 (It was 10% then) as it was just around 5% in Feb 2016. Again no sign of 'recessionary' fears justified. Unemployment was compared from last quarter in 2015 to first quarter 2016.

Unemployment Rate	First Quarter 2016	Last Quarter 2015
US	5.00%	5.10%
Canada	7.10%	7.00%
EU	10.50%	11.10%
UK	5.20%	5.60%

Key for all the tables listed below: Current =2016 and 3Months Ago= Last quarter 2015   Data Curtesy © Barchart.com

Fig 5.7 Unemployment rate

U.S Gross domestic product of a country (GDP) was positive (Fig 5.8 GDP quarterly growth). If for a country, you have two consecutive quarters of negative GDP growth, we say that the country is in recession. This is a lagging indicator. GDP, when compared from last quarter of 2015 to the first quarter of 2016, was still positive so not validating recession fears.

GDP Growth	First Quarter 2016	Last Quarter 2015
US (Billions USD)	2.00%	2.20%
Canada GBP (Millions CAD)	-0.50%	0.50%
EU (Billions EUR)	0.30%	0.30%
UK (Millions GBP)	0.50%	0.50%

Key for all the tables listed below: Current =2016 and 3Months Ago= Last quarter 2015   Data Curtesy © Barchart.com

Fig 5.8 GDP quarterly growth

U.S Wage growth in Jan 2016 was moderate.

U.S credit markets had not dried up. Interest rates and inflation was low. Interest rate was unchanged from the previous month (Fig 5.9). So, again there was no indication of recession.

Interest Rate	First Quarter 2016	Last Quarter 2015
US Fed Funds Target rate	0.50%	0.50%

Key for all the tables listed below: Current =2016 and 3Months Ago= Last quarter 2015   Data Curtesy © Barchart.com

Fig 5.9 Interest Rate

Chapter 5: Pre-Trade Analysis

During recession times, getting credit becomes difficult, hence the term credit crunch. Unemployment (Fig 5.7) starts to increase, wages stagnate and the economy comes to a grinding halt.

Low unemployment combined with high wage growth and high GDP, are signs of a strong economy. On the other hand, low unemployment, low GDP growth and wage stagnation indicate a slowing economy, whereas high unemployment, low GDP Growth and wage stagnation indicate recession, especially if you have negative growth for two consecutive quarters.

To summarise, if the US was taken as an example, then you saw that the US unemployment rate was near 5%, growth rates though showing weakness were still positive (Fig. 5.8).

Unemployment was at the lowest rate (Fig. 5.7), there was modest wage growh. Interest rates were not very high. There was no buying euphoria in the markets. All these economic indicators imply that there is no possibility of Recession in US in 2016 or 2017. Market corrections, of course are possible! You can validate further, if required, by an alternate approach like 'sector analysis'. 'Economics look to the past and markets look to the future. You should not look at one without looking at the other'.

Sector Analysis

If sectors are like waves, then industry groups are like tides that make up the waves, and stocks are like small boats that ride them. If the sector and industry group are in alignment, this will push the stock up. In Feb 2016, if you compare the 3 month performance versus 1 month performance (Fig 5.10), it shows 3 contenders for the top 3 positions – utilities, technology and healthcare. If the economy is in recession utilities, technology and healthcare will not be the current or previous top performing sectors. Sector analysis again is confirming our inference that the markets are experiencing a short-term pull back.

Considering that the U.S elections were about to take place later in the year, utilities and technology might end up outpacing healthcare. At the end of this cycle, you should expect Industrials and Financial to trend up. Financials not being at the highest for several months implied we were no where near recession and Financials and Industrials were presenting good buying opportunities. Once, U.S starts to increase interest rates it would trigger Financials to move up in the sector performance. Technology sector also looked good.

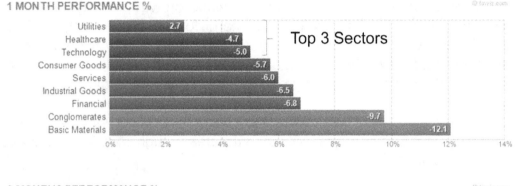

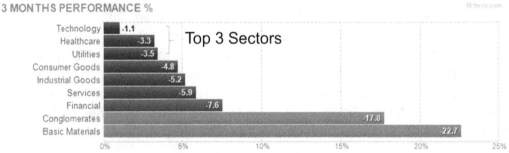

Fig 5.10 Sector Rotation

To recap on the analysis summary – the long term global outlook was weak but no contagion threat was seen. Commodity, currencies, countries' sovereign risk, slow growth, oil and China were a concern. Global growth and the US growth, was weak. The utility, technology and healthcare sectors were doing better for one reason or other. Utility was trying to reach the top. Dollar was strong. How does an investor use this information? If indices are falling, due to a company reporting poor results, then its share price will be punished accordingly.

This means in your criteria to pick quality stocks using the screener mentioned in the previous chapter you should include stocks that are generating revenue, having positive quarterly earnings, and belong to one of the three sectors – utility, technology and healthcare.

Chapter 5: Pre-Trade Analysis

Once you see next sector rotation triggered you will notice money rotating into industrials and financials. Recession fears will subside soon. Any stocks, instruments, sectors, indices, currencies or commodities mentioned in this book are not a suggestion to buy or sell. This case study is merely for education purposes only but can be used as a template for market analysis and validation.

$VIX Fig 5.4 shows a high reading of 25. If you do not have the nerves to hold during highly volatile periods, then you may have to stay in cash until such time that you feel comfortable, or until volatility returns to normal levels. Alternatively, you could include gold to balance the portfolio and select low beta stocks (A high beta stock is more volatile than the market and vice versa, beta less than 1 indicate low beta stock). As always, please remember that none of this constitutes as a recommendation. This is just for your education purpose only so that you can understand how to analyze the markets, economy and global events, to stack the probability of success in your favor. Also, this was the scenario in Feb 2016.

Now that you have reviewed market and economy, the next step is to do pre-trade analysis for a stock or share.

As an additional input to the screener, you could use volume (you want stocks that trade in high volume, and have volume in millions, not in thousands as you learnt in the strategies chapter) and pick high market capitalization. This will now give you a list of quality stocks. For each stock chart in the list, you want to look for a chart pattern, support and resistances, trend lines, Fibonacci levels, volume and pivot points. Look at entry and targets, plus comments annotated and charts saved. After this, you should perform the following additional checks:

PART 2 – PRE-TRADE ANALYSIS for Stocks

Trade Validation – Final Checks

Broker Upgrade and Downgrades

Before placing the buy order for the stock, make sure there are no broker downgrades issued on the stock that day. A downgrade means that the analyst doesn't think the stock is going to meet the expected targets. If the analyst is famous, people will sell, so watch out.

Ex-Dividend date

Some investors buy a stock just for dividends. If you are buying for dividends, you should buy well before the ex-dividend date. If the stock goes ex-dividend (this information is shown on the chart or you can search yahoo or google for the ex-dividend date) the share price normally drops in the short term. So, make sure your buy date is not on the day before the ex-dividend date.

Earnings Announcement

Some investors make the mistake of buying stocks the day before, or on the earnings announcement date, hoping to make a quick return. This is very risky. Make sure the earnings date is not due in the immediate future, preferably not within the next 2.5 months. If the earnings are bad, the company misses earnings or doesn't meet analyst expectations, the stock will start tumbling in price. You will lose money extremely quickly, because there will be broker downgrades to sell, adding momentum to the selloff. E.g. SKX Sketchers Fig 5.11.a. An uninformed investor would have got involved in buying the stock before the earnings date, and he/she would have ended up losing money. Third quarter results came out on October 22nd and the stock gapped down from $48 to $34, followed by a downgrade on the 23rd by the analyst. As a result, the stock price dropped a bit more. If only they knew not to buy a stock before the earnings date, then it could have saved the investor huge losses.

Chapter 5: Pre-Trade Analysis

Fig 5.11.a Stock price drop after poor earnings -SKX

News

As you know, bad news affects markets. Make sure there is no bad news on the stock announced on your intended purchase date.

Market Open

Do not buy a stock at the time when market opens, since you will be paying premium price. Always check to make sure that the bid and offer price difference is small with not too much variation.

Volatility

Check $VIX index, an indicator of market volatility. If the chart reads a high number of 25 or more, postpone your purchase for a low volatility day.

Risk Reward

Complete the risk reward calculations, position size, and capital allocation amount, stops, target1, target2 and target3. Risk reward calculations, trade management and money management are outlined in the coming chapters.

Annotate the Chart

As discussed in the strategies chapter; draw resistance, support and trend lines, identify patterns, volume, moving averages 50 and 200 simple moving average levels, key dates like earnings announcement, ex-dividend etc.

Confluence

If you are a beginner, have at least 3 confluences for you to make a decision to buy.

Indicator and Fitness check for the Stock

Finally, you want the stock to be fit enough to run in the direction that you want, and get a medal. In simple terms, you want the stock to run on its own track, without running around off the track (called chop, where investors lose more money because the stock keeps going up and down like a yo-yo, not really establishing a clear course i.e. in this case upwards). You want money coming and staying in the stock that you are choosing. You want more people trying to rush to buy your selected stock, and stay with it. Finally, you would prefer not to pay top price for your stock. For the fitness check, add two indicators to your chart. Add an ADX indicator to avoid sideways movement, and a stochastic indicator, so that you don't buy at a price when everyone else is selling.

1. **Avoiding chop**

    For avoiding chop you should add an ADX indicator, setting 14. If the ADX is above 25, you can say the stock is in trend. More aggressive investors are happy for it to be above 19.

2. **Buying at a price where sellers are exhausted**

    You can add an oscillator like stochastic with default settings 14, 3, 3 to make sure the stock is in the oversold area (not many sellers), generally this means stochastic above 20 and below 80. Oscillators work best in a sideways market.

Chapter 5: Pre-Trade Analysis

You need not use the indicators for buy and sell. Just use them for confluence (stacking probabilities). Fig 5.11.b is an example of how a validated chart should look, with all the annotations before risk and trade management have been completed. It should outline where you plan to enter the stock, and two or three targets. In Fig 5.11.b, General Motors on the previous resistance break at $31.48 and there is a trend line resistance break. The 1st, 2nd and 3rd resistances could be used as 3 targets. You could have exited 1/3 at T1, 1/3 at T2 and lastly 1/3 on the trend break support below 36. You could have traded this differently by committing 50% of the allocated money for this stock on the trend line break, and added the remaining 50% when T1 was pierced and exited the whole lot at T2. You could also have just traded this using price, volume and trend.

This trade had 5 confluences:

Confluence 1 – ADX>20 so not in chop.

Confluence 2 – Stochastic crossing above 20.

Confluence 3 – Trend support held.

Confluence 4 – 20 EMA crossed above 50 SMA.

Confluence 5 – A bullish engulfing candle breaking through the trend line resistance at the entry point. Target 1-$33.5 (8.5%) from entry is the first resistance, and target 2-$35.8 (15.3%) is the next resistance.

Confluence 6- Volume-At the point of entry you can see buyers accumulating the stock

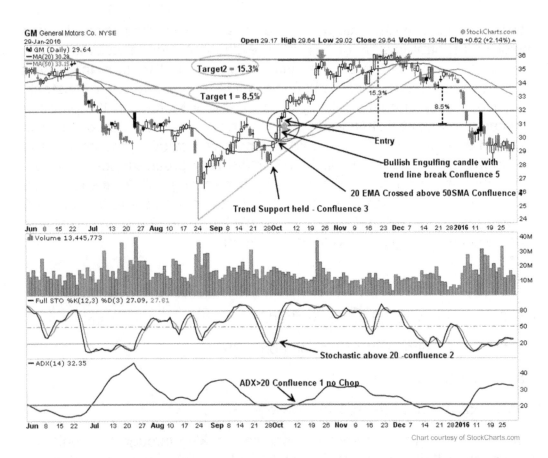

Fig 5.11.b Example chart after validation and before risk and trade management

3. Volatility indicator Bollinger Bands

This is not a must or necessary but useful. Works well on highly traded active stocks. Bollinger bands measure volatility. They were developed by John Bollinger, a world famous technical analysis trader. Bollinger bands are based on standard deviation, and are drawn with default 20,2 settings. Once drawn, you will have 3 bands – a top, a bottom and a middle band. In simple terms, as the market volatility increases, the Bollinger bands expand and as the market volatility reduces they contract. So, how can you benefit from these bands? As the price moves closer to the top of the band or pierces outside the upper band for a stock, the stock is said to be in overbought condition. If the price moves closer to the bottom of the band, or pierces through the lower band, then the stock is considered to be in the oversold condition; meaning it is good to consider buying, but make sure that you look for confluence. The other way you can use a Bollinger band is to make use of the pinch or contraction of the band in stocks. This is also referred to as 'coiling' by some traders. You could use it in conjunction with price patterns, in order to spot big moves waiting to happen, either to the upside or to the downside.

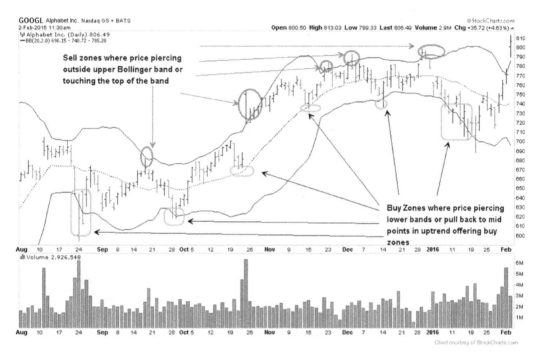

Fig 5.12 Bollinger Bands Buy and Sell zones

In Fig 5.12, the Google price chart has a Bollinger band with default settings overlayed on price. Apart from price, volume and Bollinger bands, no other indicator is added. Just in its pure form, you can see the buyzones, oversold areas and sell zones, or over bought areas on the chart. Also, shown in the chart is an advanced concept, i.e. when the stock is in uptrend (betweeen Oct 2015 and November 2015), everytime price pulled back to the mid-band, you have buying opportunities presented on Google. Of course you need to check other things for confluence, to increase your probability of success.

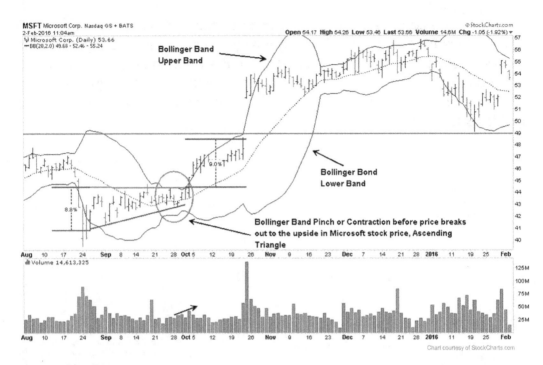

Fig 5.13 Bollinger Bands squeeze before price break in ascending triangle

In Fig 5.13 Microsoft chart, I have used a Bollinger band for high probability entry. The Bollinger squeeze indicates that a price expansion is due inside an ascending triangle. Use Bollinger Bands for confluence. Do not buy or sell solely on one indicator reading. Use patterns, trendlines, support and resistance.

Finally, use Risk Reward assesment (will be detailed in the coming chapters) for picking Good stock from bad or ugly ones. If you are a beginner, pick a stock that gives you at least $20 reward for every $10 you spend. More on this in the Risk Management chapter.

In the next chapters, you will know how professionals control risk both in the stock and in the portfolio, how to exit on profit or minimize losses.

Actions To Take

1. Find two technology stocks that went up in price after earnings, and one oil stock that went down.
2. Finalize ten stocks from your watch list.

CHAPTER 6

MANAGING MONEY

So far I have discussed how to spot opportunities, how you can select a handful of quality stocks from the universe of stocks, how to validate each stock shortlisted and how to determine targets. However, you are yet to determine where to exit if you are wrong, and how to manage your capital.

Capital preservation is the key for survival in the market.

Before you make money as a newcomer to the stock market, it is absolutely essential for you to preserve your capital. So, start investing with a small capital. Once you get good at minimizing mistakes, then you can start increasing it. Let me show you some example calculations to elaborate my point with a hypothetical scenario.

Example 1: (Fig 6.1)

Assume you have a trading capital of $200, 000. Let's say you opened 4 positions of $50,000 each. Now after several days you close three positions at 50% loss, as market turns down unexpectedly. You then have a loss of $25,000 per position and for 4 positions the loss is $100,000. Your cash in hand now is $100,000

To make $100,000 back on the $100,000 capital, you need to make 100% profit. In summary, when you lose 50%, to recover it you need to make 100% profit.

Example 2: (Fig 6.1)

Assume that you have a trading capital of $200, 000. Let's say you opened 4 positions of $50,000 each. After several days later you close these positions at 80% loss (also called drawdown) as the market turns down unexpectedly. Now you have lost $40,000 per position, and for 4 positions the total loss is $160,000. Your cash in hand now is $40,000. If you ever make 160% profit on the $40,000 capital, then you make around $64,000 profit. This will still not help you to recover your original capital.

To recover your original capital after the drawdown at 80%, you need to make a monumental 350% profit, which is beyond imagination. Top hedge fund managers make an average return of 10 to 20%. So, if you wish to recover 350%, the amount of risk you will be taking is almost insurmountable, or you need to trade leverage instruments. In search of such a high risk return, there is a high probability that your remaining capital might also vanish.

Example 3: (Fig 6.1)

On the contrary with the same capital of $200,000, if you cut your losses to 10% of the portfolio value, then you only need to make 11.12% profit to recover from it. 11.12% recovery is more practical and achievable. For this reason, keeping losses to a minimum is paramount to investing.

Fig 6.1 Percentage Profit vs Percentage Loss on $200,000 capital

Loss %	After 50% Loss	After 80% Loss	After 10% Loss
Capital Lost ($)	100,000	160,000	20,000
Capital left after loss ($)	100,000	40,000	180,000
% Profit you need to recover your original capital of $200,000	100% Gain	350% Gain	11.12% Gain

© Sankar Sharma

To manage capital appropriately, your method, system and risk management that you use must be at low risk with high reward. In other words, if your reward is $X amount and your risk is $2X, you should give this trade a miss.

To be precise, you must be clear about your maximum percent of loss that you are prepared to tolerate.

Summary:

1. Do not lose big. Big losses mean taking huge and impossible risks. Once you lose big money, psychology comes into effect and you are at risk of losing your entire capital.
2. Small losses are easy to recover. The risk is less and recovery is feasible.
3. Capital preservation is the key to sustainability and profitability.

It is best to trade chart patterns, as they have a better reward to risk ratio. Hence, I have been focusing on confluence, to increase your probability of success.

The next chapter is about risk management and position sizing (no. of units of stock to trade). Risk management is the key to achieving successful returns from your investments. Always calculate risk, and avoid trading stocks that have a reward to risk ratio of 1:2, or low reward/high risk ratio. It is best to focus on minimizing the downside risk, and improving the upside potential.

Actions To Take

Decide on your investment capital, your max % drawdown or your small loss %, in terms of capital that you can tolerate.

CHAPTER 7

MANAGING RISK

Successful investors focus on how much they could lose on a trade, and amateurs focus on how much they can make.

As discussed earlier, if you wish to have long term and consistent success in the market, capital preservation is the key. Risk management deals with the most dreaded and important aspect of your trading business – losses. This is where professionals and amateurs stand out, based on their ability to manage risk.

In the last chapter, I discussed how important it is to keep your overall loss of capital invested to minimum. In this chapter, I will be discussing how to manage loss per position or risk per position. If you keep risk per trade to a minimum, you can keep your overall loss to a minimum.

Risk management or Risk control serves two purposes:

1) To control loss per trade and portfolio loss
2) To establish whether the profit you are expecting is really meaningful in terms of risk (that you are willing to take per trade)

It is important to bear in mind that an uncontrolled loss can wipe out many winning trades. If you hear anyone mention that they wiped out or blew their trading account that means they have not understood risk management or is unaware of how to manage risk. It is most likely that they have not calculated their position sizes correctly, and do not understand the importance of this. This is often magnified when people leverage up and start margin trading. In trading, you must always know where you are going to exit from a trade, if your analysis is wrong. You need to limit your losses and maximize your profits. You need to work this out even before you place the trade. The size of the trade, the frequency of the trade and the position of stop are all variables that introduce risk into the trade. Overtrading could lead to losses, meaning that you pay repeated charges to the broker (which will eat into your capital). You must know that there is a relationship between stop loss and position size. For the purpose of risk management, I will be discussing three concepts Stop loss, risk amount and position sizing.

Chapter 7: Managing Risk

1) Stop Loss

A stop is a price level at which, if you are wrong, you would want to exit the trade. There are several ways in which investors work out their stop loss. These include:

1. Using an indicator called an average true range. At the price where they are entering the trade, people see the reading of this indicator and multiply the value by 1.5. They then deduct it from the entry price, and that is their stop.

2. Some use an indicator called parabolic stop, reverse indicator or parabolic SAR (stop and reverse). They overlay parabolic SAR on the price chart. SAR prints a series of dots below the chart, and people use this as their stop. If the price goes below the SAR dots, they exit the position.

3. Some use 9-day SMA (Simple Moving Average) and 18-day SMA, with 18-day SMA as their stop loss. If the price falls below 18-day SMA, they will exit the position, and some use 20-day SMA as their stop loss.

4. Most common place investors use stop loss is to place below the nearest support price zone or the swing low (valley) or trend line support or pivot level support.

2) Risk Amount

Risk amount is the maximum amount that you are willing to risk if your trade goes against your entry price and losses starts to increase. Some people use a fixed amount as their risk amount. Irrespective of the amount they allocate per trade, they always have a fixed amount (say $500). In my opinion, this is not a great way to calculate risk, because on a small capital you will be risking more.

For example, if you have $10,000 in your account and your risk is $1000, then your risk exposure in percentage terms is =

($1000 risk amount) / ($10,000 trade capital for this trade) = 10%

Now if you use $1000 risk on a $5000 capital, the risk exposure in percentage increases to 20%. In other words, as the capital reduces you are taking more risk. For this reason, having a fixed amount is not a great idea, even though some might use it.

Instead the method I would like to introduce to you is called '%Risk amount'. With this method as and when your trading capital per trade appreciates or depreciates, the risk amount automatically gets adjusted. For example, if you have $10,000 capital and your percentage risk amount is fixed at 3% per trade, this means that your risk amount is = 3% x $10,000 = $300. So, the maximum loss per trade is $300. Now if you have $100,000 capital, your maximum loss allowed is $3000. (This is only an example and you can vary this to suit your level of risk appetite).

At this stage you have fixed two variables, you know where the stop is going to be and how much % of your per trade capital you are risking.

3) Position sizing

Again assuming a starting investment capital of $10,000 and by knowing the stop level and risk amount, it is easy to determine the number of stocks you want to purchase i.e. position size with loss limited. For this, consider an imaginary example of xyz stock that is currently trading at $110.

Now if you purchased 1 stock of xyz at $110, and the price hits your stop at $100, you have lost **$10** or you have hit your risk tolerance of $10. This is called per unit risk or risk per share.

Capital risk for xyz stock = 3% x 10, 000 = **$300**.

The Number of xyz stocks you are going to purchase at 3% risk = Capital at Risk amount/per unit risk = **$300/$10** = 30, i.e. approximately 30 shares of xyz company. You now have to place a stop loss order in the market at the time of purchasing the stock. If the stock moves in the opposite direction, then your loss is capped at $300. (How to place your stop order is discussed in the 'Managing the Trade' chapter).

This information should give you a massive edge over millions of traders worldwide. So far I have given detailed, step-by-step information on how to minimize your loss by means of position sizing. The second application of risk management is to evaluate if a trade is worth considering, by means of reward to risk ratio.

Let me elaborate on the risk to reward ratio, as it is often called, with a couple of examples.

Example 1: Let us assume that the stock xyz is trading at a current price of $110, which is your entry price. The stop loss is $100 and your target is $115. So, if you are right about your analysis of your stock xyz then it would reach $115. That is a gain of $5 (Difference between the perceived target price of $115 and the entry price of $110).

This means your reward to risk ratio = $5 gain/$10 unit risk per trade = approx. 1:2

Reward: Risk = 1:2; meaning you are risking 2 units for 1 unit reward. Good investment? You definitely want to give this a miss.

Example 2: Let's say your target is $140, entry $110 and stop $100. So, if you are right about your analysis of your stock xyz then it would reach $140. That is a gain of $30 (Difference between the perceived target price of $140 and the entry price of $110).

This means your reward to risk ratio = $30 gain/$10 unit risk per trade = approx. 3:1

Reward: Risk = 3:1; Meaning you are risking 1 unit for 3 units reward. Good selection? Absolutely!

Now the benefit of this model is that when your amount of capital is reduced, the amount you risk also reduces, as it is calculated by percentage of the available capital. On the contrary, if the capital appreciates, your risk amount value increases accordingly. Sometimes when you are trading certain patterns, your stop loss may be more than 3%, in which case you just have to adjust your position size.

Having understood the reward to risk ratio, it is now possible for you to measure your returns in terms of risk multiples. So if you had a 3 to 1 reward to risk win, that means your profits are now thrice the amount of risk. If you move the stop, or don't place it at all and lose money, you now have a way to compute and measure how badly you lost in terms of risk multiples. This will help you to scale your next investment.

As mentioned before, you should include risk management in your pre-trade analysis, and apply it to every stock you have chosen to trade. Risk management helps you to manage your losses. Now you are well informed to place a live trade, and it is time to discuss 'trade management'.

Actions To Take
For each of the stocks in the 'watch list' work out risk and reward.

CHAPTER 8

MANAGING THE TRADE

Money management helps you to protect your investment capital, and risk management helps you to deal with your losses. Trade management or order management is focused around placing correct orders. It specifies the type of order that you need to place in order to get into a trade, the type of order you need to lock your profits or get out in profit; and the type of order that you need to cut your losses.

In other words, you need to know what order type to use, when to use it, and for what purpose. Before I continue, let me confirm what I mean by bid and ask price. If you are buying a stock then you are going to be offered ask price. If you are selling you are going to be offered bid price. The difference between ask and bid price is called spread. When the market is volatile, there will be substantial difference in the spread, ask and bid prices. You can spot this before major news, after hours, near market open or close, and in thinly traded stocks. Now let's explore the different order types.

Market Order

A market order is an order to buy or sell a share at the best available price. Using Market orders, sometimes could get you a price that is several points above or below the current bid or ask price. This happens during highly volatile periods. You should never use market orders to trade ascending, descending triangles and wedges.

Limit Order

A limit order is an order to buy a stock at or below a specified price, or to sell a stock at or above a specified price. This is a conditional order, and gets executed only if the order reaches the specified order level or a better price level. This type of order may not get executed if the specified price is not reached.

Stop Order

A stop order is a buy or sell order which automatically converts to a buy market order, and will get executed once the order is triggered by the stop price. A stop order may be placed as a day order or GTC (good till cancel) order. With a buy stop order, the price is set above the current asking price. With a sell stop order, the stop price is set below the current asking price. If the stock gaps, then the stop order will get executed, causing bigger loss than you have accounted for. To avoid this, the best possible option is to look at the history of the stock. While it is not guaranteed, if the stock had gaps in the past then it is possible that these will occur again in the future.

Stop Limit Order

This order may be a day order or good to cancel order. This is initially a stop order, but once triggered becomes a limit order. The problem with a stop limit order is that if the limit you specified isn't reached, then your order might not get executed. Use a sell stop to minimize the loss and exit the position.

To summarize, you can place a buy stop order to enter into a continuous price pattern, and a stop limit order if you are planning to enter on price rejection near support. This could be a pending order. You could use a 'sell stop order' to protect your gains or as a protective stop. You could use a 'sell limit order' above the current price at the target, to exit in profit etc.

Most online brokers have videos on how to place orders, close positions and set alerts etc. I would strongly advise you to open a 7 day demo account and practice, so that you know what to do when you go live. Most brokers are happy to guide you and give you a tour of their platform. The online broker you choose must allow you to trade in global stocks, and if not, at the very least in American stocks. You need an execution only broker, who supports stop losses. Having covered the basics of placing a trade, let me now move onto the complex subject of trade management.

Trade management is all about how you manage your stock to either profit or loss without meddling in the process. Your objective is to maximize profit and minimize loss. To maximize profit, you need a strategy that allows you to take 1/3 of your money off the table at target1. This could be the first nearest resistance, 1/3 at the 2nd target i.e. the next resistance and you let the rest run but move the stop to break even. For example, say you buy 300 shares of company xyz. You sell 100 at Target 1 and another 100 at target 2. Now you have scaled out 200 of the 300 shares you started with. The last 1/3 you can sell when the trend breaks, or using any other exit criteria triggers.

To create confidence within yourself when you are new to stock market, it is important to scale out of a position (selling some portion of shares purchased in the company xyz) at the early stages and keep locking in profits. Some advanced traders scale in their position. They place a small order and if it is working, they slowly increase their position in the winning stock.

So, how do you get targets and stops? Price patterns give you targets. For continuous patterns, the target is the measured move you know already for the pattern, as discussed in the strategies chapter. In this case, you can either take all of it when the target is reached, or you can take 1/3 halfway of the pattern, and 1/3 at the target given by the pattern. You can allow the latter to run by moving your stop to the point of entry. Of course, you will be using risk management principles to compute the order size.

At this point you know what to buy, when to buy or sell, how to maximize profits, how to minimize losses, how to control risk, how to manage your trade and how to manage your capital. In spite of knowing all of this, there is one thing that could separate winners and losers. That is your psychology or your mindset. This can make a huge difference to the outcome of whether you make profit, loss or break even. I will discuss about emotions related to investing in the next chapter.

Actions To Take
Open a demo account and for each of the stocks in the 'watch list', place entry orders and set up price alerts at the entry, stop and target price levels.

CHAPTER 9

MINDSET

Three investors can take exactly the same trade at the same entry price, and have largely differing results. One might exit in profit, one might exit in loss and one might just break-even. A big reason for this is psychology or mindset. As soon as you decide to enter the stock market and place a trade, you are entering into a den of emotions. The more leveraged your position, the more risk you place in the trade, and the more intense your emotions will be. Your results will be a direct consequence of how well you deal with these. People make good money when they are in simulation or paper trading accounts, but lose when they trade real money. Emotions such as greed, fear, ego, self-doubt, lack of confidence, lack of discipline and trust can rule your trading results. Let's examine them in detail.

Greed

If you decide that you want to become an overnight millionaire with a small capital, you are going to take on unprecedented amount of risks.

You may end up either losing the capital, or receive a margin call asking for more deposits at short notice if you are trading on margin.

Alternatively, you may decide to buy a penny stock or low volume stock that you can't sell in a volatile market, due to huge spread between your buy and sell price.

You might be in a profitable position, but because of your greed you don't follow the rules to take profits at the targets, or move stops to break even (due to lack of discipline). As a result, the price might gap down and you end up making a loss.

You might have made money on a stock, but because of greed you re-enter into the trade and commit more or all of your capital. Thus, you turn a winning position into loss when the trade goes against you. Greed is the root cause for your loss.

Fear

As a beginner you could be anxious to place your first trade, and miss an opportunity to enter a good trade. Due to fear of missing out on a trade, you might jump and buy a high momentum stock at a higher price without waiting for the pull back, or buy it without complete analysis.

You might enter the trade and realize it is showing losses immediately on your entry, as if someone is waiting to grab your money. This induces immediate fear.

You may have had a good run and everything goes fine, but suddenly there is a broker down-grade or bad news, and the stock price starts to plummet.

You might have done everything right, but global markets collapse due to some unforeseen event. Your stock keeps tumbling you don't have a stop loss order, and your losses are beyond your tolerance limit. Fear is the likely cause in all these different scenario.

Ego

You have conducted all the research and pre-trade analysis thoroughly, and you place a trade. The stock doesn't go according to plan and it is making more and more losses with each passing day. However, because of your ego, you keep holding onto it instead of cutting your losses, exiting or using stop loss. Small losses turn into big losses. In spite of several warnings that you have received, you may firmly believe that you are right and stick to the losses.

Imagine maybe because of beginner's luck on your first trade, you made 40% in four hours and now you are unstoppable. You believe you are the world's best trader and your ego says that you can beat this market hands down. On your next trade, you double your investment and ignore all the concepts of risk, trade and money management. Then the stock price drops, wiping out a huge percentage of your capital. You give back all that you made and a bit more. Now you get angry and try to recover the loss, so you take even more risk and put everything you have on the table. Suddenly, you are no longer an investor but a huge gambler. It is important to realize that Ego has caused this.

Hope

You buy a stock and now you are its biggest cheerleader. You avoid reading exit signals or the negative news and you focus only on the positive news. Dose of reality is better than two doses of hope while trading markets.

Frustration and boredom

Sometimes your stock goes nowhere and you have money tied up. Months move faster but not your stock. You sell it and the next day the stock skyrockets. It is important to remember patience pays in the stock market.

Lack of trust or confidence

Due to lack of trust in strategies, or lack of confidence in one's own abilities, you might not enter into a winning trade or exit a trade early, as the stock retraces before it goes ahead and meets the target. If this happens, start small and gradually build confidence by repetition and by gradually increasing capital as opposed to putting it all down and giving up in one single attempt.

Some of these scenarios might sound a little too dramatic, but you are bound to experience some or all of these at some stage or other during your investing cycle. Investing must not cause stress, anxiety or fear. When you are investing or trading work towards one of the three outcomes; either you exit with a maximum profit, exit with a negligible loss, or break even. This is only possible if you are disciplined enough to control your emotions and follow the rules. For this, you need rules to follow. You need a trading plan. This is what I intend to discuss in the next chapter.

Actions To Take

Write down what sort of emotions could impact your trading, and how you intend to counteract them.

CHAPTER 10

PLAN, TRACK AND IMPROVE

As human beings, we go through a transition phase before and during trading. Before entering into a trade, you will be in a rational state of mind. You'll be thinking clearly about what needs to be done and how you want to proceed. Once you have placed the trade, however, things don't always go to plan. Your state of mind becomes more emotional, as you are forced to make unexpected decisions. This is the reason why you need a trading plan. A trading plan allows you to make clear rule based decisions, instead of emotionally biased decisions. Before investing, invest time in preparing your trading plan, and then practice following it through by adhering to the rules while trading. Whenever you are emotional, the trading plan should be your go to document.

In real life, perfect execution is possible but not probable. In order to make as much money as possible, you need to perfect your trade as much as possible. This can be done by regular post-trade analysis and measuring key activities. This is where a trade journal will help you. By keeping a record of your trading activities, and by capturing feelings and emotions that helped to shape your trade, a trading journal helps you to track trading events along the way. Annotating charts is also a key part of maintaining a journal. After every trade is closed, update the journal, and conduct a post-trade analysis to see if any lessons can be learnt from that experience that you can use in your next trade. Any lesson learnt from post- trade analysis becomes a new rule, and this should be added to your trading plan. You should constantly measure your trade management, your risk management, your strategies and mindset management. Record the findings, and improve your trading to become a successful and experienced trader, with consistent returns from the market.

Now, let's look at how to create a trading plan.

Trading plan

If you have written a meticulous plan, then even someone who has never traded should be able to follow it and execute your trades without stress, and execute them to perfection.

Chapter 10: Plan, Track and Improve

Start your trading plan with the common rules that you would like to follow:

- Objectives for investing – Income or Growth or both
- Holding period – Quarter, Year, 5 Years.
- What are the markets you will be focusing on?
- Your broker(s) contact details, account login details.
- Will you be investing in large, medium or small capitalization stocks, and in what proportion?
- How much is your trading capital and what is the risk tolerance %?
- How much is your risk per trade?
- Holding decision if in profit or if in loss – are you going to hold and ride the turbulence, or exit as per your risk management rules…
    o When there is bad news?
    o When the market slumps?
    o If the trade gaps in the opposite direction?
    o Earnings miss or revenue miss or both?
    o In the event of unexpected events?
- What time (every day) are you going to conduct pre-trade analysis and for how long?
- What time are you going to review your positions?
- Where and how are you going to track the stocks?
- Where are you going to set and send alerts for your stocks?
- Where is your trading journal located? How often and when are you going to update it?
- Will you always use…
    o Support/resistance.
    o Trend lines.
    o Candlestick patterns.
    o Fibonacci.

- o Pivot levels.
- o Indicators.
- o Moving averages.

Method specific Rules for Entry

- Rules for trading continuous price pattern
    - o Name of the price pattern you will be trading.
    - o What is your key criteria for entering the trade?
    - o What will you be using for confluence?
    - o Type of order you will be using for this.
- Rules for trading reversal price pattern
    - o Name of the price pattern you will be trading
    - o What is your key criteria for entering the trade?
    - o What will you be using for confluence?
    - o Type of order you will be using for this.

Initial stop loss and trailing stops

- Rules for your initial stop loss.
- On what basis will you be trailing the stops to lock in profit?

Rules to exit the trade

- Trend line support is broken.
- Price breaks the horizontal support.
- Target is reached.
- Price gaps before reaching the target.
- When a news item is released that the market dislikes.
- When the pattern fails.

- Before earnings or ex-dividend date.
- If you have made a mistake etc.

New rules to be added based on the lessons learnt, on an ongoing basis.

Your trading plan should be used as a reference document. Refer to and read your plan every day before the market opens. When in doubt or when undecided or anxious, read the rules in your plan and follow them so that you can minimize emotional mistakes. Just like every other business, trading needs a plan.

Now, to track your plan and improve the execution of this plan, you need to review your trade activities and measure their effectiveness. You need to know strategies that worked well and strategies that failed to work. You need to know whether your stops are too tight. You need to know whether you exited too soon from a winning trade, or whether a volatile day simply magnified your losses. Did you close a winning position because you saw replay of old news and reacted wrongly? Did you fail to analyze a key facet of the trade before entering? To be able to answer these precisely, you should have registered all of the events, price points, news release times, dates, sources and your emotional reactions in your journal. Your journal will greatly aid you in measuring and improving the effectiveness of executing a trade.

Annotating Your Journal

Annotating your journal is a great way of managing and improving your investing effectiveness. A journal inculcates discipline and accountability. It helps you to spot consistencies and inconsistencies, issues with order placing and mindset issues. If you wish to improve your trading, then you need to record meticulously all the events that occurred during the trade, decisions you took along the way, your emotions, how you moved stop loss etc. This information will help you to measure the effectiveness of your decisions along the way.

Start by annotating every stock that you intend to trade. Mark the following on the charts:

- Support and resistance zones. Use green lines or green rectangles to mark support zones, and red lines or red rectangles to mark resistance zones.
- Trend lines and parallel trend lines, to spot any price channels.
- Gaps and gap up open support (mark in green), or gap down open resistance zones (mark in red).
- Vertical lines to identify any key events or news items that moved the share price, earnings and ex-dividend dates.
- The price at which you entered, place a green up arrow underneath and a small horizontal line with price point details, your stop with a small horizontal line and blue arrow, and sale point with a red down arrow. Finally, draw a small horizontal line with price point details.
- Price patterns with projected target price points.
- Reasons for entry or exit, quantity, capital invested, risk %, risk reward ratio etc.

Adding these key details will help you stay organized and focus only on decision making. It is also useful to go the extra mile, and capture these details in a spreadsheet. Recording the numbers in a Microsoft Excel spreadsheet will help you to plot data for visual inspection, or for running metrics.

Maintain a separate log to capture emotions you experience, mistakes made repeatedly and lessons learnt. If you make one mistake often. Most common mistake is moving the stop losses or not obeying rules etc. Lessons learnt goes back to trading plan as rules.

As market conditions change, performance could change, but having a journal helps you to quickly see what worked and why. Even the best investors experience performance deviation and maintaining a journal is the only thing that can help you to keep track and improve performance. Write about the markets, what you learnt on that day and write about your discipline, decisions and emotions.

Chapter 10: Plan, Track and Improve

So far, in the journal you have learnt to capture activities and events during pre-trade analysis, risk management, trade management, and money management etc. but to improve you need to conduct post-trade analysis. For post-trade analysis, you need to know what to measure and the key metrics.

Measure to Manage

To be successful at investing, you have to be consistent in your results. This will come by minimizing your mistakes. But how do you know what is contributing to your losses? Is it your methods, is it your mind or is it your trade management? What is your strongest point when it comes to trading? Are you following your rules and waiting until your stocks meet their target or are you snatching your profits and letting your losers run? Unless you actively measure you will not know. You start with measuring every single aspect. As you start to become consistent, you can reduce the number of things you measure to a few key aspects, which might affect 80% of your result. Fig 10.1 gives you the base to start with, and you can amend this as you feel fit for your trading.

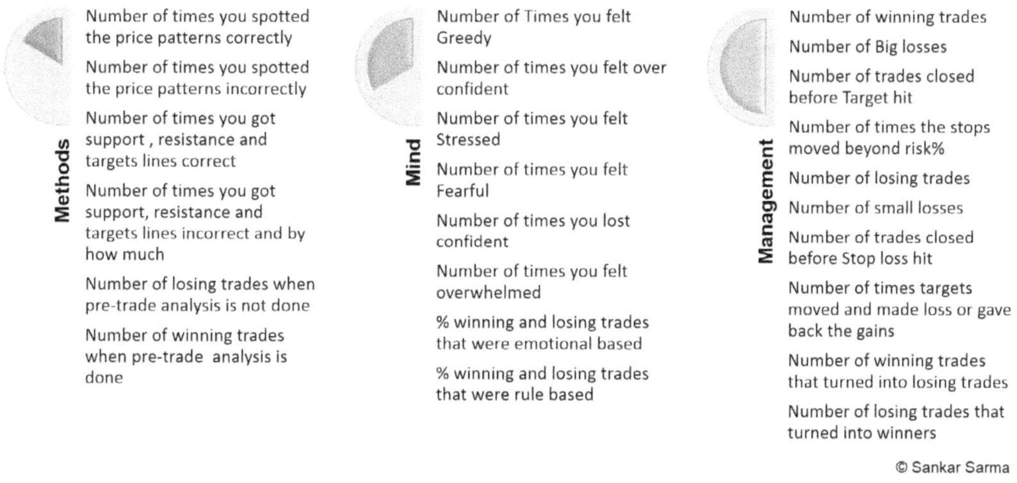

Methods
- Number of times you spotted the price patterns correctly
- Number of times you spotted the price patterns incorrectly
- Number of times you got support, resistance and targets lines correct
- Number of times you got support, resistance and targets lines incorrect and by how much
- Number of losing trades when pre-trade analysis is not done
- Number of winning trades when pre-trade analysis is done

Mind
- Number of Times you felt Greedy
- Number of times you felt over confident
- Number of times you felt Stressed
- Number of times you felt Fearful
- Number of times you lost confident
- Number of times you felt overwhelmed
- % winning and losing trades that were emotional based
- % winning and losing trades that were rule based

Management
- Number of winning trades
- Number of Big losses
- Number of trades closed before Target hit
- Number of times the stops moved beyond risk%
- Number of losing trades
- Number of small losses
- Number of trades closed before Stop loss hit
- Number of times targets moved and made loss or gave back the gains
- Number of winning trades that turned into losing trades
- Number of losing trades that turned into winners

© Sankar Sarma

Fig 10.1 Track your strategies, mind and management

Post-Trade Analysis

Market is the biggest tutor. It teaches you a lot during your investing career. However, you need a way to capture these teachings and improve your trading. This is where post-trade analysis plays an important role. You can learn a lot more from a position that made you a loss, than one that made you a profit. So, once you have closed your position or sold your holdings of a share, it is important to go back to your journal and review your decisions at each stage. This will allow you to see if your decisions were emotionally driven, or rule based. How well did you stick to the rules, or did you deviate from them? Did you use the plan? Rate your discipline, was your analysis good or bad? Take each trade you made and measure how well you managed your strategies, mind and finances. Once you have reviewed these factors, write in your trade plan specifically what you should start doing, stop doing and continue to do. Update your trading plan accordingly.

Actions To Take
Start writing your own trading plan and include post-trade analysis routine. Update your plan as you find new rules to add.

CHAPTER 11

ACHIEVE STOCK MARKET SUCCESS

Having completed the last chapter, you are now well equipped with valuable lifetime skills that can help you to succeed in the stock market. Firstly, you are aware of the important tools that will help you to determine:

- Where to 'enter' with high probability, points of confluence, support and resistance, trend lines and channels, stochastics, Bollinger bands, Fibonacci etc.
- Where to 'exit' with clear target objectives or measured moves (price patterns), candlestick patterns, Bollinger bands and stochastics.
- Volatility using Bollinger bands.
- When not to enter in a trade, chop zones to avoid losses using ADX indicator and reversal price patterns.
- Stop losses to minimize your losses or exit break-even when wrong.
- Quality stocks, stocks that are worth considering, stocks that can give high probability returns using risk vs reward.
- How to execute an order, how to place an order to buy or sell, or a stop loss order to cut your loss and exit in profit.

Secondly, at any stage if you are lost, not knowing what to do, then you know that you can start with the simple 4 step process of identification, validation ,execution and measure performance.

Lastly, I have attempted to minimize the unknowns by increasing awareness, so that you know how to spot opportunities and control risk in both in your portfolio as well as the share you purchased.

In a nutshell, you now have all the steps and processes needed for you to achieve low risk and high rewards.

As I come to the end of my book, there are a few final words of wisdom that I would like to share.

Practice what is discussed, spend more screen time, learn discipline, dedicate time, be consistent and learn from your mistakes to improve. Do not enter the investing world with greed. You will only become a slave to fear. Instead master the methods discussed, perfect the trade execution and be disciplined. Discipline is what separates the professional from the novice.

If you master and excel in discipline, then consistency will come in search of you. You must be disciplined enough to do pre-trade analysis, disciplined enough to keep your emotions in control, disciplined enough to follow risk management and trade management guidelines, disciplined enough to follow and execute your plan, and disciplined enough to measure and improve your skill. Only then you can achieve consistency in your trade executions and returns. Maintain tenacity and do not break the rules of investing. Improve along the way!

CHAPTER 12

AFTERWORD

Irrespective of when this book gets published the methods, strategies and principles mentioned here can still be applied for analysis in the years to come. They are not specific to the year of writing or publication. It is important to note that this book is supported on www.RiskRewardReturn.com with constantly updated material.

Any stocks mentioned in the book is not a recommendation to buy or sell. Depending on when you purchased this book the economic conditions might have changed. So you would need to re-evaluate the scenario using the principles and case studies mentioned as a guide.

After several hours of debate it was decided to publish this book with black and white charts. This is primarily because we wanted the cost to be minimal for our readers and make it affordable to anyone who wanted to learn about stock market investing/trading. Colored charts are available for download on the associated website www.RiskRewardReturn.com at no extra cost to you. Enter your First Name and Primary Email Address to get access.

Tell us how the book helped you with your trading. We would love to hear about your success stories. You can send them to support@RiskRewardReturn.com.

CHAPTER 13

BIBLIOGRAPHY AND REFERENCES

INDEX

A
aggressive entry, 28, 54
ascending triangle, 54, 55, 56, 86, 110
ask price, 11, 120

B
bar charts, 21, 69
Bar charts, 56
beta stocks, 103
bid price, 11, 120
Bollinger bands, 108, 109, 134
Bollinger Bands, 110
bullish candles, 21

C
candlestick chart, 21, 22, 34
capital, 7, 9, 14, 48, 106, 112, 113, 114, 115, 116, 117, 118, 120, 122, 123, 124, 125, 128, 131
channel trading, 36
close price, 20, 21, 74, 81
confluence, 29, 36, 38, 42, 44, 46, 47, 48, 67, 78, 80, 86, 87, 106, 107, 108, 109, 110, 114, 129, 134
congestion or rectangle pattern, 65
conservative entry, 26, 28
Continuous price patterns, 50

D
descending triangle, 54, 57
dividends, 7, 104
Dow Jones Index, 9
Down Swing, 26
downgrade, 90, 103, 104, 124

E
ETFs, 11, 12
ex-dividend, 104, 106, 129, 131

F
FCA, 8
Fibonacci, 30, 42, 43, 44, 76, 78, 86, 103, 128, 134
Flags and Pennants, 51
FTSE 100, 52, 87

G
GDP, 100, 101

H
head and shoulders, 75
high price, 20, 43

I
index, 9
Interest rate, 100
Inverse head and shoulders, 64, 65, 67
investor, 7
IVEM process, 12

J
journal, 13, 15, 16, 93, 127, 128, 130, 131, 133

L
Line charts, 21
low price, 20, 29

M
Managing money, 14, 112
managing risk, 14, 18, 115
mindset, 15, 18, 122, 123, 130
Moving averages, 78

N
NASDAQ 100 index, 10, 87

O
open price, 20, 23, 45, 81

P
peak, 24
Pivot point analysis, 44
position size, 106, 115, 117, 118
post-trade analysis, 15, 132
pre-trade analysis, 14, 15, 87, 88, 89, 90, 103, 119, 124, 128, 131, 135
primary trend, 32, 50

R
resistance, 20, 31
reversal pattern, 50, 67, 75, 81, 83
risk management, 18, 113, 114, 115, 117, 119, 120, 122, 127, 128, 131, 135

S
S&P 500 index, 10
SEBI, 8
SEC, 8
secondary trend, 32, 42
Single Bottom, 69
stock exchange, 8
stop loss, 13, 15, 49, 50, 70, 86, 115, 116, 117, 118, 124, 129, 130, 134
stop order, 50, 51, 54, 117, 121
Strategies, 14
support, 20
SWOT, 90, 91, 92, 94, 97, 98
Symmetrical triangle, 58

T
Technical analysis, 20
trader, 8
trading plan, 14, 16, 125, 127, 128, 130, 131, 133
Trading volumes, 77
trend lines, 30, 31, 35, 38, 47, 49, 51, 62, 92, 93, 106, 128, 130, 134
Triangle Price patterns, 54
Triple or Multiple Top, 74
trough, 24

U
Up swing', 26

V
Volatility index, 92, 95

W
Wedges, 62

About the Author

Sankar Sharma is an author, investor, mentor and founder of RiskRewardReturn.com. With a graduate engineering degree and a masters in Finance, he has had the splendid opportunity to research and test most advanced trading strategies with Wall Street veterans.

Based on his experiences and insights into several indicators, he has developed a unique method of investing and trading called the 3R system which uses the principles of managing Risk, Developing a winning mindset and practicing discipline to achieve success in the stock market. The methods described in the 3R system have been tried and tested using Stocks, Derivatives, E-minis, Fx markets and Commodities.

Over the years, Mr. Sharma has been trading with some of the best Investors, Traders and Hedge Fund Managers. Having amassed a vast knowledge in trading g Stocks, Derivatives, E-minis, FX markets and Commodities, he wanted to share his experiences and train newcomers in the investing market. So he decided to write a book on how to trade in the stock market that will act as a guide and provide a complete end-to-end process that is easy to follow.

'Stock Market made simple' is intended for all aspiring investors and traders to help them keep guess work at bay and minimize the time spent on research and analysis. The book highlights the importance of being objective while trading, to be accountable for one's decisions, to be disciplined and minimize risks in order to maximize returns.

Mr. Sharma provides consultation for individuals, Institutions and conducts training seminars for investors and traders.

More details regarding the author, his training programs and the 3R group is available at www.RiskRewardReturn.com

Chapter 13: Bibliography and References   153

Useful Resources @ RiskRewardReturn.com

1. Access Coloured Pictures of 'Stock Trading Made Simple'

All the charts and pictures depicted in the book can be accessed at the below website for FREE.

https://www.riskrewardreturn.com/MyBooks

All you need to do is enter your first name and your primary email address to access it.

2. References and Recommended Reading

List of recommended books and references are listed here. Visit below to find out -

https://www.riskrewardreturn.com/MyBooks

3. Additional Benefits

i) Courses Available At RiskRewardReturn.com

These courses are designed to give you momentum and guided learning. All these courses are built using the unique 3R System (Risk Reward Return Methodology).

Learn At Lunch Series

Are you a beginner and do you find it difficult to allocate time to learn how to invest in the stock market? Then this course is for you. Allocate 15 minutes learning for 4 days a week and in 3 months' time you will have thorough knowledge of how to invest in the stock market.

Learn Stock Trading

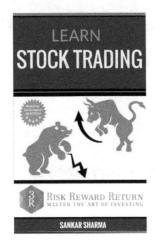

Are you a detailed person who wants to know all your options on the table and choose the best that fits your style? Then this course is for you.

This is a complete end-to-end course where students can learn trading in stocks. This course is for those who are eager to complete the program in a short period of three days and who are hungry to learn all the advance strategies. This course provides deeper learning of several strategies. You can pick and choose the one that fits your style. Find out more about this and all other courses on the web site.

Quick Start To Investing - How To Invest Your First 1K

This is a Foundation course where you can learn one simple strategy and how it can be used again and again. It is a detailed and step-by-step course for someone looking for less complex and more effective ways to invest in the stock market.

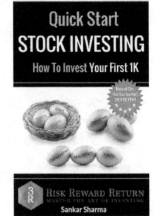

Discover these and many more useful programs by visiting https://www.riskrewardreturn.com/

ii) Discount Offer

An EXCLUSIVE DISCOUNT OFFER for the readers of this book

- On any course @RiskRewardReturn.com site that costs between $500 - $1000 Claim a $100 discount using the code BOOK24
- On any course @RiskRewardReturn.com that costs $2000 or above

  Claim a $200 discount using the code BOOK42

Please check the website for terms, conditions, disclaimers and privacy policy. These offers may be altered or removed at any time with little or no notice. These offers cannot be combined with other offers as they are mutually exclusive.

CPSIA information can be obtained
at www.ICGtesting.com
Printed in the USA
LVHW101422080420
652652LV00006B/128